Save the Last Bullet

Save the Last Bullet is a true story of a German boy-soldier coming of age at the apocalyptic end of World War II. In the powerful tradition of *The Red Badge of Courage* and *All is Quiet on the Western Front*, it will haunt and inspire. Fast paced, frightening, and heart pounding, beautifully written, an unforgettable read.

James McMurtry Longo, Ed.D
Author *Hitler and the Habsburgs: The Fuhrer's Vendetta Against the Austrian Royals*

Save the Last Bullet

Memoir of a Boy Soldier in Hitler's Army

Wilhelm Langbein with
Heidi Langbein-Allen

Pen & Sword
MILITARY

First published in Great Britain in 2022 by
Pen & Sword Military
An imprint of
Pen & Sword Books Ltd
Yorkshire – Philadelphia

Copyright © Wilhelm Langbein with Heidi Langbein-Allen 2022

ISBN 978 1 39907 239 7

The right of Wilhelm Langbein with Heidi Langbein-Allen to be identified as Author of this work has been asserted by them in accordance with the Copyright, Designs and Patents Act 1988.

A CIP catalogue record for this book is available from the British Library.

All rights reserved. No part of this book may be reproduced or transmitted in any form or by any means, electronic or mechanical including photocopying, recording or by any information storage and retrieval system, without permission from the Publisher in writing.

Typeset by Mac Style
Printed in the UK by CPI Group (UK) Ltd, Croydon, CR0 4YY.

Pen & Sword Books Limited incorporates the imprints of Atlas, Archaeology, Aviation, Discovery, Family History, Fiction, History, Maritime, Military, Military Classics, Politics, Select, Transport, True Crime, Air World, Frontline Publishing, Leo Cooper, Remember When, Seaforth Publishing, The Praetorian Press, Wharncliffe Local History, Wharncliffe Transport, Wharncliffe True Crime and White Owl.

For a complete list of Pen & Sword titles please contact

PEN & SWORD BOOKS LIMITED
47 Church Street, Barnsley, South Yorkshire, S70 2AS, England
E-mail: enquiries@pen-and-sword.co.uk
Website: www.pen-and-sword.co.uk

Or

PEN AND SWORD BOOKS
1950 Lawrence Rd, Havertown, PA 19083, USA
E-mail: Uspen-and-sword@casematepublishers.com
Website: www.penandswordbooks.com

For Papa

Contents

Acknowledgments   xii
Author's Note   xv
Prologue   xvii
The Hitler Youth   xx

Part I: Foreshadowing   1

Chapter 1	Brenken, August 1934	3
Chapter 2	1935	9
Chapter 3	1936	14
Chapter 4	1937	18
Chapter 5	10 November 1938	20
Chapter 6	1939	24
Chapter 7	1940–1941	25
Chapter 8	1942–1943	30

Part II: The Führer Takes Care of Our Children   33

Chapter 9	Konstanz	35
Chapter 10	The Vollmars	41
Chapter 11	Christmas 1943	50
Chapter 12	The Hitler Youth	58
Chapter 13	Military Training	60

Chapter 14	Schleching	64
Chapter 15	The SS	70
Chapter 16	*Heldentot*	76

Part III: Total War — 85

Chapter 17	The Last Bullet	87
Chapter 18	The Retreat	94
Chapter 19	The Barbed Wire Incident	100
Chapter 20	The Ceasefire	104
Chapter 21	The Internment Camp	112
Chapter 22	The Long Road Home	119

Part IV: The Aftermath — 131

Chapter 23	The Reunion	133
Chapter 24	Expectation Meets Reality	142
Chapter 25	Onkel Franz's Farm	154
Chapter 26	The Occupying Forces	159
Chapter 27	Sunday Mass	162
Chapter 28	The Bootlegging Incident	165
Chapter 29	Mischief with Fritz Freudewald	167
Chapter 30	The Fire Brigade	169
Chapter 31	Return from the Farm	174
Chapter 32	Holding Pattern	181
Chapter 33	The Path Forward	189

Epilogue — 198
Bibliography — 200

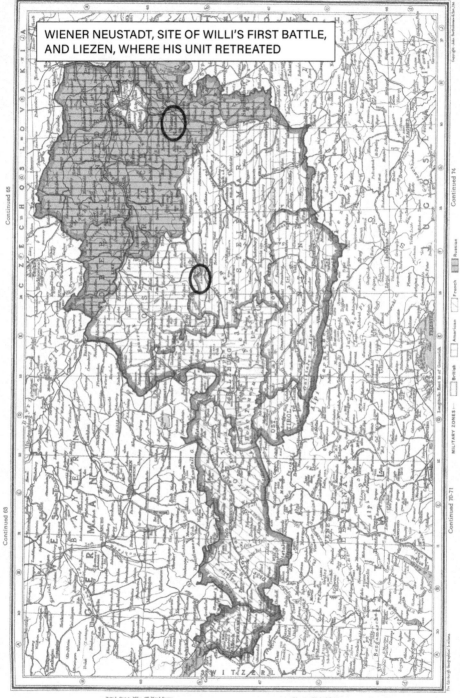

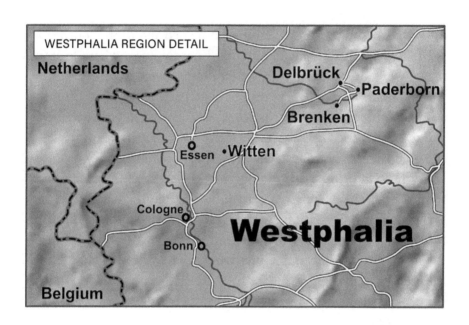

Acknowledgments

There are so many people who helped me in my journey to make this book a reality that I hardly know where to start. I want to extend my deepest gratitude to:

My father, whose story this is. He patiently entertained my millions of questions right until his passing. His integrity, honesty and sense of justice inspired me to strive to become the best person I can be. I hope to honour his memory by publishing this book.

My husband, John, who lovingly and steadfastly supported me from the very beginning and patiently tolerated my long hours and absorption in my work that took so much time away from him. He knew it was important to me. He is my rock.

My children, John and Gina, who always encouraged me and believed in me every step of the way. They were my sounding board when I doubted myself, and my cheerleaders when I needed encouragement.

My mother, Teresa, who shared important memories about my father that provided deeper insight into his past and who is the keeper of all pictures and documents. She is my private librarian and has fascinating stories of her own which deserve to be told.

My sister, Graziella, with whom I share the unique bond of sisterhood and of growing up with our parents. She understands everything like nobody else can.

My uncle, Paul Schuette, who generously shared family stories, pictures, and memories, and who sent me valuable bibliography about my father's – and his – home town of Witten. The postage bill to ship those books from Germany to the US must have been frightful.

My dear friend, former colleague and fellow writer, Mark Jackson, who nudged me in the right direction when I didn't know what I was doing – and kept nudging – and without whose unwavering faith in my abilities I probably would not have become a writer. I have much to learn from him yet.

My writers' group friends, Peggy Lang, Jim Riffel, Tim Kane, Cary Lowe, Lee Polevoi, Cameron Harrison and Jack Innis, whose expert advice and critique so significantly improved my work. Special thanks go to Peggy, for her extracurricular help when I needed it, and for her instinct to know when I needed her help; to Tim, for his map-making skills; and to Cary, for generously and unconditionally offering his assistance and expert insights, and for introducing me to his publisher.

Tracy Jones, my editor, for greatly improving the manuscript and getting it into publishable shape. She is always spot on. I could not have done it without her guidance.

Marni Freedman, for teaching me the craft of writing, an invaluable gift, and for giving me excellent advice about seeking agents when I didn't know I should.

My fellow memoir class students, for the amazing stories and experiences they so openly shared. I became a better writer for it.

My beta readers, for taking on the task, for their kind words, encouragement, enthusiasm, support and, above all, friendship. All are incredibly dear to my heart. A heartfelt thank you goes to Adrienne Behrens for her stimulating conversations and impeccable command of the English language which made me rethink the choice of some words. Thanks to Peter Heavey for contributing the word 'disabuse', which has a history of its own and has a special place in the manuscript, and for introducing me to his friends, Brian Carlin and Heiko Hiemer. Thanks to Brian for the sharpest proofreading yet, and for helping me improve the title. Thanks to Heiko for our conversations in German, for urging me to publish the book in German because it has to be so, and for introducing me to his friend Gisela, who had original and intriguing observations and helped me correct the names of German localities. Lastly, thanks to Steve Weyer for his longstanding mentorship and friendship going back many years, and for his kind and generous words that boosted my morale.

Myra Fagg, for developing my website and for being so patient, kind and supportive.

Pedro Ribera, for putting me in touch with a Spanish publisher.

My dear friend Paul Cheall, creator of the top-rated Second World War podcast www.fightingthroughpodcast.co.uk and narrator extraordinaire, who enthusiastically took on the project of airing an excerpt of my manuscript and broadcast it to the world with unparalleled skill, and for introducing me to his publishers, Pen & Sword, who have become my publishers. I am forever in his debt.

Brigadier Henry Wilson, commissioning editor of Pen & Sword, for taking a chance with a first-time author and believing in my book. His friendship is very dear to me.

Rita Rosenkranz, my agent, who saw the potential in my manuscript and took a personal interest in it.

My friends Maria Jesus Plasencia and Karen Cop, who have been in my life for a very long time and know me so well; Karen, for providing advice, encouragement and connections; Maria Jesus, for generously helping me with the significant task of translating my manuscript into German and Spanish in her own time.

All my friends and family for being there for me. Every one of them helped me along the way. I am forever grateful.

Author's Note

After I pestered my father for years to record his memories as a child soldier in the Nazi army, he finally agreed and narrated his story, in German, on cassette tapes, converted them to audio CDs and sent them to my sister and me in 2007. When I got them I listened to them once and, feeling I had somehow accomplished my goal, forgot about them for the next nine years. In 2016 the realization set in that my father was eighty-six years old, one of the last surviving soldiers of the Second World War. He lived in a nursing home and was not doing well. How much time did I have to ask him any more questions?

Over the next year and a half I made weekly phone calls to my father and interviewed him as much as I could about his story. He willingly agreed to talk and was pleased that I expressed interest and wanted to know more. Unfortunately, his health was rapidly declining, and he, who had always had a prodigious memory, could not recall certain things any more. I could sense that some memories were too painful for him. I did not want to press him and make him relive the trauma of war in the twilight of his life just to satisfy my curiosity, not unless he volunteered the information. Sometimes, when I asked him a probing question about the war, he would become very quiet and, eventually, he'd say in a soft voice that seemed to come from far away, 'I don't remember.'

Nevertheless, I was able to fill many gaps in the taped recollections of the harrowing experiences that so deeply traumatized him. In the process, I came to understand that his emotional distance as I was growing up was a wall he had built to bury his pain. To move forward, he needed to contain it behind a dam.

I tell my father's story in his own words, without judgement or apology. His is the report of an eyewitness and unwitting participant in the horror of the Third Reich, seen from his perspective as a child.

Some creative licence has been taken with dialogue and scenes, as the original conversations and events were not always described in detail by my father. I have tried to render them in the spirit of how such encounters are likely to have taken place, or the way in which the events may have unfolded, based on memories of conversations with my father or my own observations growing up. Several people's names have been changed to protect their privacy, as have the names and descriptions of certain places.

Heidi Langbein-Allen
Escondido, California

Prologue

I called Papa on Sunday morning for our weekly chat, which he had come to expect. It was evening for him at his retirement home in Spain. He picked up, and I spoke to him in German.

'Hi, Papa, how are you today?'

'*Kampfstimmung!*'[fighting mood], he declared.

Kampfstimmung. That single word summed up how he defined his entire life. First, he fought in the Second World War, the war that robbed him of his childhood, then he fought his family and his country, who denied him permission to grieve and work through the trauma of war. Along the way there were the obstacles he overcame in his professional life – the nay-sayers, the envious, those who declared he wouldn't make it. But he persevered. Brilliant, unapologetic and brash, the straight-shooter who would tell it like he saw it whether or not you wanted to hear it continued to stubbornly plough his way through life, daring anybody to oppose him, never giving up.

I laughed. 'Okay, then can I ask you some questions?'

'Sure, fire away.'

'I'd like to pick up where we left off last week. Tell me more about your first battle.'

'Ah, yes.'

He paused as if to collect his thoughts. Then, in a distant voice, he started telling his story.

* * *

Austria, Wiener Neustadt, 31 March or 1 April 1945

We stood in the holes we had dug at a distance of about 10 metres from each other. In each of them there was a man, or a fourteen-year-old boy like me.

Each of us had four *Panzerfäuste*, anti-tank rocket launchers, at his disposal. The transport truck for the *Panzerfäuste* was a short distance behind us, so we could get more in case it became necessary, because it was a disposable weapon and could only be fired once. If you fired your four *Panzerfäuste* and more tanks were coming, you better had run back to the truck to get replenished.

My fellow soldiers and I stood in our holes and waited in oppressive silence. Nobody spoke. Time was passing too slowly and too quickly, all at the same time. I knew a battle was coming and that I might die, but my brain was too jumbled to formulate the great thoughts that I imagined one should have in those moments. The minutes crawled by as I felt a vein pulsing in my neck. Somewhere in the back of my mind, a tiny voice was admonishing me that I was running out of time. To do what I was not sure; maybe to live? But I couldn't focus on that because we had a job to do. Fear was something we could not afford.

Then I felt it. The deep rumble, the growl in the earth under my feet, pulsing its way up through my bones. Soon the tanks appeared, their dark silhouettes materializing just over the horizon. I grabbed a *Panzerfaust*. The Russians had a famous tank, the T-34, the most versatile tank around. It could run over anything. Father Stalin had given his soldiers excellent weapons, we had been told. Now I could see them first-hand. There were so many.

The wall of tanks rolled inexorably closer, partly obscuring the sky. As they approached, I saw the Russian grenadiers marching behind the tanks with their bayonets pointing straight ahead. The T-34s started getting within shooting range. I raised the *Panzerfaust* on to my right shoulder, tucked it under my armpit and looked through the viewfinder to locate my target. The weapons instructor's words played back in my head:

'Let the tank advance to a distance of exactly twenty metres from you, no more, no less.' *You only get one shot at this.* 'At twenty metres your shell will penetrate the hull of the tank, any further and you will miss.' *No time left to grab another weapon and aim it.* 'Any closer, you won't have time to shoot anymore.' *Even if you shoot, it will run you over.*

I glanced at the 20-metre mark I had previously located in the field in front of me to estimate the tank's distance correctly. It was a whitish boulder. *Close, they're close.* I squared my stance. Right eye on the viewfinder, left eye shut. I zeroed in on the tank directly in front of me. A drop of sweat stung my right eye. I blinked furiously. *Shit.* Home in again. *God, it's big.* The tank reached the white boulder. *Steady. Steady. Now!* I pulled the trigger. The shell blasted off. I held my breath.

The Hitler Youth

The *Deutsches Jungvolk* (DJ) was a Nazi youth organization for boys between ten and fourteen years old. After that came a transfer to the *Hitlerjugend* (HJ), or Hitler Youth, which took boys from fourteen to eighteen. Once they reached eighteen years of age, they transitioned directly into the armed forces. The Hitler Youth aimed to indoctrinate children into National Socialism, train them to pledge allegiance to Adolf Hitler and provide them with pre-military training. The organization was part of the National Socialist strategy of *Gleichschaltung*, controlling all areas of life. Its objective was to condition youngsters to an unthinking acceptance of the system and to the renunciation of any independent political and social will.

The second implementing Regulation (Youth Service Ordinance) of the Hitler Youth Act of 25 March 1939 made membership in the *Deutsches Jungvolk* mandatory. *Jungvolk* activities were quasi-military in nature, and group activities took place on weekday afternoons, Saturdays, and Sundays, purposely reducing the time children spent at home. Members were required to take a test on subjects which included knowledge of the German anthem and the Hitler Youth flag song. New entrants also had to be able to recite Hitler's life story in about six to ten sentences.

In 1939 Rudolf Benze, the director of the German Central Institute for Education and Instruction, declared that control over education was held by the National Socialist movement alone, allegedly in the name of the people. The family, ethnic associations and private interests came second, and only under the supervision of the NSDAP, the Nazi party. He further stated that parents were to be replaced or had to be educated if the insufficient or faulty guidance of their children made it necessary.

Part I

Foreshadowing

Chapter 1

Brenken, August 1934

'Opa, Opa, can we go find water today? Pleease?' I begged, jumping up and down to get Opa's attention.

Opa [grandpa] Johannes had special abilities. He could, with his bare hands or with a rod, find water under the ground. He was a *Wasserforscher*, a dowser. His skills were known all over the small village of Brenken in the Westphalia region of Germany, where he had lived all his life. I loved spending time with my Opa. My many cousins, all older than me, would run out and play in the barns, but I, just four years old, would ask Opa if we could go out to find water in the fields while he told me stories. It was Saturday afternoon, the eve of my grandparents' golden wedding anniversary celebration. My parents and I had just arrived at the farm from the city of Witten, where we lived, when I ran up to Opa.

'Opa, Opa, can we go? Please, please?' I insisted, tugging at his trousers. He laughed heartily, a belly laugh that shook his slight but wiry frame. He pulled up his braces, tucked in his white shirt with the sleeves rolled up to his elbows, adjusted his black trousers over his worn boots, grabbed his hat and his divining rod and stretched out his left hand, sporting an impish smile and a glimmer in his eye.

'*Komm*, Willi, let's go find us some water.'

'Okay, Opa,' I squealed, grabbing his hand, and tugging him to the door, lest he change his mind at the last minute.

The thunder and lightning of a summer storm had stopped a little while ago, and the heavens were pulling back the leaden curtain that had dropped sheets of water on us all morning, revealing glorious sunshine and a bright azure sky, dotted here and there with puffy white clouds that looked like cotton balls. I was itching to go out, and with Opa, what a treat!

As we walked out of the door, he said to me, 'You carry the rod. I will tell you where to look and when you think it's twitching you give it to me.'

My eyes grew big. That was a great responsibility I had every intention of faithfully fulfilling. I picked up my pace to keep up, for I was still little, and Opa was quick-footed. The earth was wet, and the sweet aroma of the plants that grew in the meadow wafted into my nose. I took a deep breath, and a spring found its way into my step. I skipped forward along the unpaved trail, humming a little melody.

'There, Willi, there on the left, by the cat's tail, let's go there.'

'Okay, Opa.'

I rushed over to the tall, skinny, bright green plant that did look so much like a scrawny cat's tail and spotted some big snails on it. The silvery trails they left behind as they climbed their way up the plant glistened in the sun. They were lumbering up the branches, carrying their houses on their back, antennae straight up in the air. I couldn't resist, I lightly tapped one antenna, and whoops, it was gone. I giggled and tapped another one.

'Look, Opa, they are hiding in their houses,' I exclaimed, turning to him.

'Yes, yes, they do that.' He smiled at me and his face lit up, making me feel warm inside. 'Well, let's see if the rod twitches around here.'

Solemnly, I handed him the magic instrument. He took hold of it and pointed it at the ground, walking slowly straight ahead. I walked at his side, mesmerized by his concentration.

'Opa, are you sure you are going to find water?'

'Yes, of course, Willi. Of course, eventually I will,' he assured me.

'And Opa, do you think one day I could find water too?' I asked, filled with hopeful anticipation.

'Why, yes, you can find water too.'

He looked at me with affection and took my little hand in his big calloused one, weathered by a lifetime of hard farming labour.

We had stopped walking. We were standing in a wheat field, bathed in the golden glow of the late afternoon sun. I looked up at him in wonder.

'Are you sure?' I asked doubtfully, fervently hoping he was right but fearful that maybe he wasn't.

Opa squeezed my hand.

'*Ja*, little Willi, yes, I am. It's easy. You can do anything. You just have to believe you can.'

* * *

'No, Willi, stop. You stop at once!' Mama's voice carried far.

Oh, oh, I'm in trouble.

I lay face down in a puddle of mud outside the pigsty; I had tried to catch the cute squealing piglets, but they were faster than me, and I had accidentally slipped. It wasn't my fault the ground was so slick, and I had almost caught one. My Sunday church outfit was a little stained.

'*Ach, mein Gott*, what are we going to do now? Your clothes are ruined,' she wailed as she approached.

I looked at her in puzzlement while rubbing mud out of my eyes and nose, wondering why she had a big frown on her face. It wasn't a big deal, just a little dirt.

'But Mama, I almost caught the piggy.'

'I told you we were taking Opa's and Oma's golden wedding anniversary photograph. Everybody is there already; the photographer is waiting. This is a disaster – you come with me right now.'

She started walking hurriedly but awkwardly, fruitlessly trying to avoid the mud puddles staining her nice dark blue satin heels and splashing dirt on the below-the-knee pleated navy-blue skirt she had especially picked out for the occasion.

I followed, crestfallen, my shoes squishing uncomfortably with every step.

'What's a photograph, Mama?' I yelled after her, trying to keep up.

My mother just shook her head and stomped forward.

'Just walk, Willi, hurry, for heaven's sake. But don't touch me.'

I was hurt. *Why doesn't she want me to touch her? She must be really mad at me.*

Opa Johannes Hardes and Oma Maria had twelve children, six boys and six girls. For their golden wedding anniversary all the children had gathered at the farm with their respective spouses and most of their offspring to take a photograph in commemoration of the event. That was a lot of people, and they were all waiting for me.

Mama rushed me into the house through the back door and up the stairs to our room. She ordered me to strip down to my underwear and rubbed me down with a cold and wet *Waschlappen*, a washcloth, which she had dunked in the enamel washbasin that was sitting on the dresser. I yowled in outraged protest.

'Hush, be quiet. You are making us so late with your mischief. What will Papa think?'

I stopped squirming. I did not want to upset Papa, as I did not want to get a spanking.

In record time, Mama squeezed me into a clean white shirt with a round collar, lederhosen, long white socks and leather booties, scooped me up and flew down the heavy wooden winding staircase to the living room. Everybody turned to look.

'Maria, where have you been?' demanded Papa in a stern voice.

Mama was flustered.

'Willi ran off to the pigsty and got all muddy; I had to clean him up,' she said, catching her breath. Her cheeks were flushed and her chin was raised, a little defiance in her stance. She put me down. Papa stiffened and gave me a fulminating stare. When Papa got upset, people took notice. It was best to keep out of his way. I cringed, looking for a safe place beyond his reach.

'All right, everybody please take their places.' The photographer started giving sharp instructions. 'The anniversary couple in the front, sitting down, grandchildren at their feet, and the adult children with their spouses in the back. Ladies next to their husbands, stand slightly at an angle but look at the camera.'

I scampered to the front and took my place among my five older cousins. For some reason they had me sit in a chair next to my oldest cousin, also named Willi, who was busy pushing his younger brother Hans.

'Hey, Willi, where were you?' Cousin Mia asked me.

'In the pigsty. I almost caught a piglet. You want to come and catch one later?'

Her eyes widened, and she nodded vigorously.

'Children, please stay still,' barked the photographer.

We looked up, astonished at this strange contraption we had never seen before. He was putting his face behind a box with a hole in the middle which sat on a tripod. One of his hands was holding some kind of tray. It made no sense to me at all.

Finally, everybody was in place, all thirty-one of us, in the large living room of the ancestral farm which Opa, the firstborn son, had inherited from his father, and he from his. This farm would be passed down to Onkel Franz, Opa's eldest son, when the time came. The midday light that streamed in through the large windows brightened the room. All twelve children, six redheads and six with raven-black hair, with or without spouse and children, stood poised to immortalize the occasion. The wooden floor was polished to a spotless shine for the occasion, and the only piece of furniture in the frame of the photograph was a small round wicker table on which my Opa rested his hand. Opa looked quite dignified in his black suit with his First World War medals on his lapel. Oma, at his side, was clad entirely in black, in permanent mourning for her eight children who had not survived childhood, a large gold crucifix pin on her chest the only adornment she allowed herself. The old couple sat straight in their chairs, proud to be accompanied by all their adult children and their families in this moment, a lifetime of hard work behind them. I looked at them, amazed that Opa and Oma were so much smaller than my aunts and uncles, and wondered if people shrank when they got old.

The photographer hid his face behind the box, then raised his right hand over it, holding a contraption on a cord.

'Everybody, look at the camera and stand completely still. On the count of three. One. Two. Three.'

He squeezed the contraption in his hand. There was a flash of light and a noise, and it was done. We had been immortalized in a photograph, whatever that was. I was unimpressed.

'Is it over yet?' I asked, squirming in my chair, my neck itchy from the scratchy starched shirt Mama had made me wear.

'Get going. Go to the kitchen to get some snacks. Do NOT go outside,' shouted our mothers.

We all looked at each other in utter disappointment. As I ran to the kitchen behind my cousins I turned back and saw Mama. She was looking at me, smiling. Oh, good. I was not in trouble after all.

Chapter 2

1935

Something had gone wrong at my birth, and my mother had almost died. While recovering at the hospital, the doctors gave her the bad news that she would never bear children again. She was devastated. She came from a family of twelve and a long line of Catholic farmers who considered large families a gift from God, aside from being welcome help on the farm. Luckily, I was a boy, thereby preserving the male line, at least saving my mother from the anguish that would have ensued had she not been able to produce a male heir.

However, my mother's heart was secretly set on having a little girl. She couldn't help herself. She let my hair grow into a little pageboy cut and dressed me in outfits that looked suspiciously like dresses, although she maintained they were tunics or overalls, until I was about three years old, when she couldn't get away with it anymore. My relatives jokingly told me more than once that I made a very pretty little girl. They seem to have found the whole business quite amusing.

Mama was often sick. Her ailment was never fully discussed or explained. It was something to do with a bleeding disease, which would cause her to haemorrhage. She would faint and could not take care of me because she was bedridden for days at a time. I suspected it had to do with whatever happened to her when she gave birth to me, which was also only ever mentioned in hushed conversation. On those occasions when she was ill, from when I was a baby to shortly before enrolling in primary school, I would be dropped off with the neighbours, the Rosenbaums, who owned a shoe store in town. I spent so much time with them that I came to consider the Rosenbaums my second family. They had a little boy, Fritz, just over a year old. Frau Rosenbaum also watched another neighbor's boy, and we played together, little Fritz in tow. We would make elaborate tent fortresses in Fritz's room by stringing sheets from the top bunk bed and attaching the other end to furniture.

'Halt. Who goes there?' the 'Lord' would demand from inside the 'fortress'.

'It is *Ritter* Valiant Heart; I need shelter for the night,' the petitioner would respond.

Invariably, some challenges would have to be overcome to gain access. In the end, all of us would end up falling asleep on the floor in the tent, and Frau Rosenbaum would carry us to our beds and tuck us in.

It was usually Papa who dropped me off in the morning at the Rosenbaums on his way to work at the *Reichsbahn*, the German national railways. Like all railway personnel, Papa was a government employee, which meant that by default he was a member of the NSDAP, the National Socialist German Workers' Party (Nazis), since government workers were automatically enrolled.

All party members were required by the authorities of the Third Reich to provide Aryan race credentials. The concept of an Aryan race was a construct the Reich had created to identify a 'pure' race, superior to all others. An Aryan was not allowed to have any Jewish ancestry. Consequently, Papa had to prove his family's non-Jewish heritage by producing baptismal and marriage records of his and Mama's parents and grandparents. If he couldn't prove racial purity, at least to their grandparents' generation, rumour had it that unpleasant consequences might be in store for us.

Papa was worried. When he was young, his parents had told him stories about a Jewish ancestor. Now he needed to find out if these stories were really true and, if they were, how far removed the ancestor was from his generation.

As a child, Papa remembered his Oma, Anna Kalle, telling him about her grandfather, a Jewish merchant from Portugal who followed the Napoleonic army on its way to invade Russia in 1812. The Emperor Napoleon travelled from Paris to Moscow with his *Grande Armée*, hundreds of thousands strong, on a path that took him straight through Germany. The village of Delbrück, where my paternal grandmother's ancestral home stood, was on that route.

According to the story, when passing through the village with Napoleon's troops, Kalle suddenly thought better of going to war and decided instead to settle there. Legend had it that among his belongings was a trunk filled with gold ducats. There was speculation about where the treasure had come from, and theories were floated that he had made his money in Africa, then sailed to Portugal and made his way north aiming to tie his fate and fortune to that of the great Emperor Napoleon. But, so the tale went, my grandmother's ancestress happened to catch his eye as he passed by, at which he fell helplessly in love and married her.

Papa went to the Delbrück Catholic church, which had records going back to the seventeenth and eighteenth centuries, to check marriage and baptismal registers. There, he discovered that in the early nineteenth century there had indeed been the marriage of a man named Kalle to a Delbrück resident. The name did not appear anywhere else in the church records prior to that entry, meaning he had to be a newcomer to the village.

And then there was the matter of the trunk full of gold ducats. This trunk was sitting in our family room, filled with Mama's linen instead of gold which, if it had ever existed, had long since disappeared. The trunk had metal reinforcement bands running from back to front. According to an art expert I consulted long after the war, the trunk dated back to the correct period, and its metal strips represented the Israelite army's battle formation, lending further credence to the family stories and the evidence of the church records.

Papa went to city hall with all his findings, as required of him. Given that the records showed this mysterious ancestor as his great-grandfather, he was able to prove his Aryan ancestry to his grandparents' generation. It was concluded by the authorities that any Jewish blood flowing through my father's veins was diluted enough and, to his great relief, the matter was closed.

* * *

The way the Kalle trunk, of considerable historical value, ended up sitting in my parents' family room storing linens was a fascinating story of its own.

Papa on his father's side came from a long line of stoic Prussian merchants. My paternal great-grandfather Wilhelm hailed from the eastern province of Saxony, where he owned the Langbein chemical factory. In an astonishing move, shrouded in mystery, he and his brother suddenly decided one day to move. Nobody remembered or perhaps ever knew the true reason why, but they settled in the Westphalian city of Paderborn, far to the west. There he married a woman who was the sole heiress to a considerable fortune. The couple were extremely happy together and had several children. Great-grandpa Wilhelm was no longer a young man when he married and, suddenly finding himself quite rich after a lifetime of hard work as an entrepreneur, decided that he did not want too much to do with work anymore and dedicated his time to riding around town in a Landau carriage drawn by two horses. Unfortunately, he was, as contemporaries described him, 'not free from lustiness and frivolity,' a condition that caused him eventually to squander his wife's fortune. The result of it was that his son, my Opa Wilhelm, having been left no money, was forced to earn an honest living, which he did by taking up the old family trade, chemical works. In contrast to his father, an obvious anomaly in the family tree, he was a serious man who focused all his efforts on his chemical dye factory.

Opa Wilhelm married Anna, the descendant of the Jewish merchant Kalle, whose trunk she used to transport her dowry to her new home. And that became the trunk's job. When Papa got married to Mama, his parents gave him the trunk to offer as a present to his new bride so she could transport her dowry to her new home.

I loved to jump on that trunk and pretend I was a cowboy riding on a horse in the wild Wild West, under the watchful eye of the walrus-moustached Opa Langbein posing with Oma Anna, both of whom looked benevolently down at me from their picture on the wall.

'Yeehaw, giddy up, horsy!' I would cry, taking inspiration from radio shows that told stories of cowboys and Indians.

Papa would glance up at me from his newspaper, looking over his glasses with a half-amused expression stealing across his face. But, not wanting to betray any mirth, he would sternly warn me: 'Stop making a ruckus, Willi, I can't hear myself think, for the love of God.'

Chapter 3

1936

The kerchief on my neck was itchy, and I squirmed on my perch on top of the trunk.

'Willi, please hold still. We are taking your picture in one, two, three,' said the photographer.

It was my first day of school. I was a young entrant, having just turned six a few days before. It was a momentous occasion that families always celebrated with picture-taking. My photograph was being taken at home sitting on a trunk, wearing a nice dark green tweed suit consisting of short trousers, long white socks with pom-poms, short black lace-up boots, a hunter's jacket with black velour lapels, and a neck kerchief in the Tyrolean style. As was customary, a small blackboard was placed at my feet, on which was written 'Willi's first school day'. It was also traditional for each child to receive a large, colourful cardboard cone filled with sweets on this special day, and I posed for a second picture with the cone in my arms. I was so excited about the adventures that awaited me that I didn't even think of eating the wonderful sweets. When I got back from school, Opa Johannes was at the house. He had travelled all the way from the village for the celebration of my first day of school.

'Opa! Opa!' I shouted when I saw him, running up to him and hugging him tight.

'Hello, hello, little Willi. Congratulations on your big day,' he chuckled, hugging me back.

'Wait, I have something for you.'

I sped off to my room and rushed back, slightly flustered, carrying my cone. 'Here, for you and Oma,' I beamed, shoving it into his arms. I was elated at being able to give my Opa something so grand.

He smiled and gently patted my head.

'Thank you, my boy, Oma and I will enjoy this very much,' he said with a little wink, and together we walked to the dining room for our celebration dinner.

My school was the Catholic elementary school for the boys and girls of Witten. I was a quick learner and eagerly took to reading and writing. I couldn't wait to go to this exciting place every day and play with my new friends. We learned the Nazi salute and practised it every morning when our teacher walked into class. We stood up tall, right arm raised straight and high in front of us, and shouted in unison, 'Heil Hitler!'

The schoolbooks were colourful and had stories like 'Father tells us about the Führer'. In this story, Father said about the Führer, 'He brought us home to his nice, big house called Germany. This is why, boys and girls, you must promise him again today that you will always be his loyal helpers. To our beloved Führer Adolf Hitler! *Sieg Heil!*' [Hail Victory] Mother was shown sewing Father's *Sturmabteilung* (SA) uniform, the dress of Nazis' original paramilitary wing, while Father talked to the children.

'Surely, this is what your parents tell you at home, don't they?' our teachers would ask.

We all nodded emphatically. I nodded not because I experienced that at home – although we had a picture of the Führer on the wall, which was mandatory – but because I knew that was the right thing to do; everybody else was doing it, and it made the teachers happy.

* * *

Aside from finding water and telling supernatural stories, Opa Johannes also had the special gift of foresight. He had visions nobody could explain that accurately predicted the future. One night in 1936 he had a powerful vision in which he foresaw the Second World War. He told the townspeople of Brenken: 'People, watch out, a tragedy is going to befall Germany. There will be a great war under which Germany will suffer terrible evil.' People were critical of him, but he stood steadfastly by his vision. This certainty was to cause him trouble.

Opa was not a member of the NSDAP, but his neighbour, the farmer Koppenburg, who had a farm as large as his, was a party official exempted from military service who wore the brown pseudo-uniform of the civilian party officials. Men like him were disparagingly referred to as *Goldfasane*, golden pheasants, to signify that they were superfluous ornamental fluff. Koppenburg did not like Opa's talk of impending doom because it threatened the image of the party, so he set out to make Opa pay for this transgression. Koppenburg lodged a complaint against him with the NSDAP's *Ortsgruppenführer*, the local party leader, alleging that Opa cheated on the weight of produce he sold in the market. This led to my grandfather being paid a visit by the local authorities, who audited his business. Apparently, they were unable to find any wrongdoing, and the matter was dropped. But the message had been sent; maybe next time they would find something.

My Opa died later that year. He suddenly fell sick and never recovered. Mama was sitting at the family room table with red-rimmed eyes one day when I came home from school. She called me to her side and told me, 'Willi, I have sad news today. Your Opa is gone; we have lost him, and he is in heaven now.'

'Why is he in heaven, Mama? Is he coming back?' I asked, alarmed.

'No, he's not coming back. It was his time to go because God called him to his side. All of us will be called by God one day, and we will have to go,' she replied, tears welling up in her eyes.

This news stunned me. The world as I knew it had permanently changed in an instant. The security I had felt in my little universe was false, and I did not know how to deal with that. I felt as if the ground was moving under my feet, and I started crying. Mama took me in her arms and began to sob as she rocked me back and forth.

After the funeral in Brenken we attended the traditional Westphalian wake held at the farm. Oma had passed away a year earlier, but I had not understood her 'leaving' as clearly as I had Opa's departure, in part because Oma had been mentally absent, and I had never developed a relationship with her. She was a shadowy figure for me who ended up fading away completely. Opa was a different story. I adored him and felt his absence keenly.

At the wake, all the relatives gathered to celebrate the life of the departed, and massive amounts of food and alcohol were consumed. These affairs typically lasted all night, and everybody got drunk. This time was no exception. The deceased had to receive a proper send-off, and Opa was well respected in the community, so not only were his twelve children with spouses and offspring there, but most of the village as well.

'Why are people happy that Opa died?' I asked Mama, puzzled and saddened by the lively conversation and laughter at the table.

'They are not happy, Willi. They are just remembering Opa in the way that he would have liked, with stories and laughter.'

That kind of made sense to me. I went to sleep remembering the fun times when my Opa took me on adventures to find water and we'd find so many other things along the way, bugs and plants, rocks and dirt paths that led nowhere. And during those long walks he would tell me fantastic stories that I didn't always understand but which never failed to fire up my imagination. I felt better knowing Opa would always be with me.

Chapter 4

1937

Being an only child and the male heir placed a heavy burden on me from an early age. Only the best would do, and I had to excel in everything that I did. Papa made that abundantly clear. He was also a disciplinarian, so convinced that a firm hand at home bred a disciplined mind that he would preemptively belt me every morning before school, once across the buttocks, because according to him, I was bound to do something that deserved it during the day while he wasn't around. Resigned to my fate, I assumed the position every morning, knowing that it wasn't going to hurt that much. He could have whacked me a lot harder, but his heart must not have been in it. I decided it was more like a formality that had to be checked off the list to maintain good order. And, I figured, I kind of deserved it at least half the time.

My parents took a keen interest in my education and liked to leaf through my schoolbooks, wanting to understand what their child was being taught and curious to compare the books with those from their own school days.

We were all sitting at the family room table one afternoon. I was doing cursive writing homework, which was still taught in the elaborate *Suetterlin* style with long, arched letters that required an artistic talent I did not possess. Mama was reading the introductory paragraph of the test booklet, issued in 1934.

She read out loud: 'Children are a gift of God, and an adornment and a source of happiness for the parents. Therefore, the education of their children is the most important and the most sacred duty for parents. The school will help the parents with this important task and, through parental discipline and planned instruction, will mould the children into worthy and useful members of the family, the community, the State and the Church.'

'This is so true, Joseph, isn't it?' she said, pausing after the paragraph with a satisfied sigh.

'Yes, Maria, that is correct, as it should be,' nodded Papa in agreement, leafing through the introduction to the German Elementary School Reading Book. 'Here, let me read this introduction; it's newer than the one from your book, it's from 1935, and it's from the Führer.' He read:

It is through German parents that God gave us life. He gives us our bread from German soil. Blood and soil, the people and the homeland are the hands of God, from which we receive everything that we are. Never do we want to let those hands go. We want to hold on to the German homeland and be one with our German people. Heil Hitler! Berlin, 18 June 1935.

He picked up another textbook and read the introduction.

'Here, Maria, listen, another preface by the Führer: "He who wants to live, fights, and he who does not want to fight in this world of eternal struggle, does not deserve to live." And this challenge to our boys: "You must be quick as the greyhound, tough as leather, and hard as Krupp steel."'

Papa looked up and exchanged a quizzical look with Mama that I did not fully understand. I could not tell how he felt about what he had read, but it seemed to give both of my parents pause. I looked up at them, expecting to hear their comments, but nothing more was said. They looked down and continued to quietly read the schoolbooks.

Chapter 5

10 November 1938

'Papa, what's going on?'

Papa and I were walking to the train station where he worked. The dawn sky had an orange glow. It was a strange colour and it seemed to come from behind the buildings in the distance. There were faint noises I did not recognize, but they didn't sound right. I slowed my pace a bit, but Papa pulled my arm, walking faster. His hand gripped mine so tightly it hurt. It scared me.

'Hurry, Willi, quick, let's go. There is something going on here in which I don't want to get involved.'

I wanted to ask more questions, but the intensity in his voice made me keep quiet. We kept walking briskly along the road. Papa was taking me to his workplace that morning before dropping me off at school. He didn't explain why; he just said he had to stop there first. When we got to the station, it was abuzz with activity despite the early morning hour. Trains were waiting, their bellies filling up with morning travellers on their way to work. Loud announcements about arrivals and departures were made, conductors paced up and down the platforms, shrill whistles warned travellers a train was leaving the station. Papa rushed me to the back office, where he worked, towards the end of the first platform. He was an *Oberlagermeister*, the manager in charge of all baggage consignments at the *Reichsbahn*. His rank was sufficiently high for him to have his own office.

'Sit here, Willi. I'll be right back,' he said, motioning with his hand to a chair behind an empty desk.

'All right,' I replied, putting down my Rucksack and sitting at the desk.

Papa didn't completely close the door behind him as he had intended to do when he left the room, so I was able to make him out through the narrow opening. He was talking to somebody in hushed tones.

'… burned down … dragged them to the fields …,' I heard a man say. I didn't dare get up and disobey Papa, but I craned my neck and listened harder, anxious to find out what was going on.

'Where are … ?' Papa asked.

'… at the hospital … more damage …,' came the reply.

'… safe?' Papa's voice again.

'Yes…,' was the muffled response, or so I thought.

Papa pushed the door open rather abruptly, startling me.

'Willi, get your things. Let's go, or you'll be late for school.'

I grabbed my Rucksack and followed Papa out of the door, across the Arrivals hall and back to the road by which we had come. Papa looked preoccupied. I wondered what that conversation had been all about.

When we turned the street corner to get to my school we walked into a completely unexpected and chaotic scene of firemen dousing the remains of a fire at the building right next door to the secondary school for boys, the one to which I would transfer from primary school in a couple of years. The building was Witten's synagogue, now reduced to a smouldering ruin. The firemen yelled at some older kids who were trying to get into the wrecked building to nose around. Teachers were on their tail, stepping into the smoking rubble to pull them out and march them back into the classrooms. I just stood there, mouth wide open, aghast at the sight before me and not fully comprehending it.

'Willi, stop staring, come on, let's keep walking,' urged Papa impatiently, pulling my sleeve. 'I thought he said it was safe,' he blurted out under his breath.

'Papa, what happened here?' I asked, stunned.

'Nothing. I don't know, son. I really don't know,' Papa replied, hanging his head and shaking it as if he were trying to rid himself of a cobweb. We walked past the burnt-out building and made our way to my school. When we got there, Papa left me on the front steps.

'Go on now. I'll pick you up after school.'

He turned around and hurried off. I just stood in front of the door for a moment, feeling a queasiness in the pit of my stomach.

Only much later did I realize that I had witnessed the early morning aftermath of *Kristallnacht*, the Night of Broken Glass, when thousands of Jewish businesses and hundreds of synagogues were vandalized or burnt down by angry Nazi mobs all over Germany, allegedly in outrage over the murder of a German diplomat by a Jewish extremist. But in 1938, at eight years old, I received no explanation from my parents about what was happening. Nevertheless, catching only snippets of whispered conversation here and there, I began to notice that something was amiss.

* * *

Papa came home one evening after attending a mandatory NSDAP town hall meeting and started a hushed conversation with Mama in the family room. I was in my room but I could hear almost everything they said as the walls were very thin. I was surprised by their whispers, which made me instantly curious.

I heard Papa say, '… group leader lamented that certain citizens continue to take their money to the Jew, instead of supporting the honest German merchants … said that the last word has not been spoken yet on this matter.'

'That's nonsense,' I heard Mama hissing. 'Telling me where to buy my shoes. Who do they think they …?'

'Hush, Maria, you're going to invite trouble.' My father's voice came through a little stronger.

'But Julia is my friend...' The muffled voice of my mother trailed off.

I walked into the room, and my parents acted as if they were busying themselves with something that demanded their full attention.

Chapter 6

1939

Mama and Papa were glued to the radio, turning the dials and trying to get clear reception to hear the Führer's announcement. Germany had invaded Poland. France and England had declared war on Germany, and German troops were being deployed to defend the Fatherland. They sat in silence, taking in every bit of news. The radio was playing constantly from that point on. The Führer could be heard making speeches, and announcements were made of glorious victories as the German armies advanced inexorably eastwards, gaining what the Führer called *'Lebensraum'*, the living space necessary for the German people to expand their population.

Mama was worried about Papa getting drafted into the war, but fortunately he was not a good candidate. He was a decorated First World War veteran who had fought in the trenches of Verdun, and he was a government employee working in a critical industry, train transportation. He was also older and, by virtue of his government employment, a member of the Nazi party. I couldn't help but feel that, despite all the exalted war talk on the radio, which announced the inevitable victory of the German people, and despite his big talk with his friends at the dinner table – 'We're going to shoot a piece of dynamite up these English plutocrats' arses,' I heard him say to an approving audience – Papa was not really telling the truth about how he felt. There was something about the way he looked at me when he thought nobody was paying attention that made me uneasy. His mouth was set in a thin line, his jaw tight. He looked afraid.

Chapter 7

1940–1941

The day of the induction test had arrived. Everybody was on edge.

My classmates and I graduated to the *Oberschule für Jungen*, the Secondary School for Boys, after completing the fourth grade in 1940. At the same time, we were also automatically enrolled in the *Jungvolk*, the Hitler youth organization for boys between the ages of ten and fourteen. Our names were communicated to the authorities, and we received an invitation to join.

Membership was not optional. Irrespective of the fact that every boy was automatically and mandatorily enrolled, and that nobody was left behind no matter what, part of the enrolment process included an examination in which we had to recite important facts of Hitler's life ('Adolf Hitler was born on 20 April 1889 in Braunau am Inn …'), as well sing the German anthem and the Horst Wessel hymn ('Raise the flag! The ranks tightly closed!'), and so forth. It would be utterly mortifying to fail this test, not to mention embarrassing to our parents. We would never be able to live it down.

'Do you know the songs?' asked my friend Kalla Klatsch, wiping his forehead with the back of his hand.

'I do. I have them all memorized. Do you?' I said, trying to appear confident, my sweaty hands betraying me.

'Nope. I just can't retain all the lyrics.'

He looked at me with a nervous frown.

'Don't worry, you'll be fine. Papa said we get admitted even if we don't know everything perfectly.' I told him.

He shot me a doubtful glance, but it seemed to calm him down a little. And off we went to take the exam. After a few false starts and some stuttering, all of us managed to muddle through, and as expected, we were all accepted into the corps.

Boys in the *Jungvolk* transitioned to the *Hitlerjugend*, the Hitler youth, at fourteen years of age. At the age of eighteen, young men entered compulsory military service, which in wartime was of indefinite duration. There were equivalent organizations for girls, the *Jungmädelbund* for the younger ones, and the *Bund Deutscher Mädel* for the fourteen-to-eighteen-year-olds. Greenhorns like us were known by the nickname *Pimpfe*, which meant 'small farts' and made plainly obvious our rock-bottom status in the organization. Advancement was achieved by earning badges and winning challenges.

We had magnificent uniforms, which we wore to school on the days we had after-school activities. I was enormously proud of my uniform. It gave me the feeling that I belonged to an important organization. It consisted of the *Braunhemd*, a brown shirt which had long sleeves but could be worn with the sleeves rolled up, black shorts, a belt, a neckerchief, a leather strap worn across the chest, and a field knife which had the colours of the Reich, red, white and black, etched on its handle. The field knife and the cross-strap had to be earned by overcoming various physical fitness challenges. I was keen to acquire them and set out to beat every challenge so I could earn them quickly.

Jungvolk was exciting. We played sports and outdoor scouting games in the neighbouring fields and woods. There was one game I loved. We formed two teams, one carrying a red kerchief in their trouser pockets and the other, a blue one. One team would hide and leave hints and clues for the other team, the pursuers. The pursuers' goal was to find all the opposing team members within a certain amount of time. Whenever a kid was found, he was tapped on the shoulder three times and had to give up his kerchief. Once all the kerchiefs were collected, the game was over. I was rather good at finding people and routinely managed to find my friend Kalla Klatsch, who always seemed to end up on the opposing team.

'Oh, man, not again,' sighed Kalla, the umpteenth time I found him hiding behind a large log and tapped him on the shoulder.

'Sorry, pal, hand over the kerchief,' I grinned, collecting the item.

Hanging his head, Kalla started walking toward the starting point, then turned around.

'I'm out of here. See you later. Do you want to walk home together?'

'Yeah, after I kick some more arses over here,' I chuckled.

Kalle rolled his eyes and left.

Another field game we played was a simulation battle, in which we learned to throw dummy grenades made of wood. We would dig foxholes, then opposing teams threw the grenades at each other and collected points every time one hit the mark and 'blew up' an enemy. Of all the activities, however, my favourite was shooting practice. They took us to the range to practise target shooting with air rifles. The target was a cut-out figure of a man with the heart marked as the bull's eye. We received high praise for hitting the target, and as I had an outstanding eye, I was often shown to the others as an example to follow. At the end of practice we would line up, and the instructor called out the top three marksmen. I was almost always first.

'Look at Willi, that's the way to do it. This is the way we show the enemy we are superior and how we bring them to their knees. This is the quality of the elite troops we produce, that the world fears and that make our Führer proud – Heil Hitler!' the instructor used to shout.

We would snap to attention, right arm raised, and shout back in unison, 'Heil Hitler!'

I felt three inches taller every time I heard my name called and saw the admiring looks the others gave me. It made me want to improve my skills even more.

The activities were scheduled every Wednesday afternoon, as well as Saturday and most Sundays. This meant I could not attend church regularly anymore, which did not make me too sad, because the *Jungvolk* events were much more fun than sitting in a church service. We didn't get to have many family outings anymore either, since we were so busy with the organization. The mock military drills and marches increased in frequency, and we were told that soon our turn would come to have the privilege to serve our Führer and our country in battle. We were giddy with excitement at the prospect that we would soon be real soldiers, like the grown-ups in the newsreels who were winning all the battles for the Fatherland and getting shiny medals.

'I can't wait to kick some Tommies' arses' or 'Let's give the Frenchies what they deserve', one or the other kid would announce, everybody else hooting and hollering in response.

As time went on, it seemed we were spending less and less time with our families without really noticing, like the frog in the pot of simmering water who doesn't realize he is boiling until it's too late.

I hadn't been to my little friend Fritz Rosenbaum's for a while, but I hadn't worked up the nerve to ask my parents why. I was afraid to ask because I thought I had figured out the answer – I couldn't go to his house because his dad was a Jew. Frau Julia Rosenbaum was Christian, but Herr Fritz Rosenbaum was Jewish. The synagogue burning down, an incident of vandalism at the Jewish cemetery I had heard about, my parent's hushed discussions, the fact that people didn't go to Jewish stores anymore: all pointed to it. Because these disturbing events lingered in my mind, I started noticing things, like the stars that Jewish people had started wearing on their sleeves.

'Papa, why do Jewish people have to wear that yellow star on their sleeve?' I asked him one late afternoon while doing homework at the dining room table, trying to sound casual.

I was attempting to make sense of it all, but more than anything else I hoped to get a lead-in to asking about my friend Fritz.

'Well, so people will know they are Jews, of course,' he retorted, peering up from his newspaper and over his spectacles with narrowed eyes, clearly annoyed at my asking such an obvious thing.

'But why do people have to know?' I insisted.

'Boy, mind your homework and stop asking stupid questions,' came the sharp reply from behind the paper.

I held my tongue. I knew that pressing further would lead to a belting and nothing more. It just didn't make any sense to me. I thought of Herr Rosenbaum having to wear that thing and wondered how it made him feel. He was so nice and good-natured; he always had a smile on his face and kind words to say to everybody. I couldn't understand why people needed to know that he was a Jew, like it was a bad thing.

Chapter 8

1942–1943

By 1942, when I was twelve years old, the war had become fully visible to me. The English were aggressively bombing German industrial cities. Witten had not been the target of too many raids yet, and at night the air-raid sirens we heard were typically warning of bombing in the neighbouring cities of Dortmund, Bochum or Wuppertal. These places were not far from Witten, and we could clearly see the air raids unfolding in the sky. It was a mesmerizing show, like bright fireworks. First, we saw the sky light up with so-called Christmas lights, red and green flares set off to spot enemy planes. Then we could see the planes, and the flak soldiers firing the anti-aircraft guns at them; sometimes the planes fell out of the sky. The anti-aircraft guns fired tracer that followed the aircraft. The play of lights was eerily beautiful to see, but what lurked behind that beauty was the inescapable knowledge, even to us children, that while the lights were fascinating to watch, their purpose was destruction, and the consequences were counted in human lives. And yet, I couldn't fight the irresistible attraction of looking at the deadly play of lights, like a moth drawn to a flame.

On a nice summer Sunday, right after church, we were in our backyard, which had a small garden area with a metal bar from which Mama hung her rugs to beat the dust out of them with a solid wicker paddle expressly made for the purpose. I was helping her beat a rug when the air-raid siren went off.

'Hurry, Willi! Run!' Mama shouted, wide-eyed.

We scrambled down a flight of stairs to the coal cellar, together with the rest of our neighbours in the apartment building who were all piling in to take cover. The small dark cellar had been fitted out with a couple of planks resting on breeze blocks to serve as makeshift benches. It was also equipped with the requisite sand-filled bucket and shovel to extinguish fires, as well as a bucket of water and a contraption consisting of a stick with a bunch of rags tied on one end of it, to be used to put out sparks. Only a sliver of light filtered through a tiny obscured window.

We huddled in silence. Nothing much was said, everybody was preoccupied with their own worries. Mama was quiet, too, head bowed, hands in her lap as if in prayer. I sat close to Mama, very straight, lips pressed tight, hoping nobody could hear my heart beating like crazy in my chest, betraying my fear. I was embarrassed by feeling afraid; I was supposed to be tough and strong, the future of the Reich, as we were told by our *Jungvolk* leaders. It would not do to be scared. Besides, I was supposed to protect Mama. What would she think if she knew?

This time it was only ten minutes until we heard the 'all clear' signal. We were grateful for that, as it could take so much longer. We left quietly and resumed our interrupted chores as if nothing had happened. Air raids had become part of everyday life.

Die Kinderlandverschickung (*KLV*)

To protect against the threat of ever-increasing air raids and because of serious supply issues in cities, about 2 million children were evacuated to rural areas of Germany until the end of the Second World War. The 10- to 14-year-olds were taken with their classrooms and placed in about 9,000 different outposts in the country. The National Socialist propaganda machine invested a great deal of effort in portraying the *Kinderlandverschickung* (KLV) programme as health-giving vacation trips for city children. This emergency situation gave the Nazis an opportunity to further pursue their strategy: the children would be protected from the war and simultaneously exposed to political and ideological indoctrination as well as to paramilitary drills, while removed from the influence of their parents and the church and settled in surrogate homes, boarding houses and youth hostels.

The programme was touted as voluntary. However, after insufficient parents responded to the advertising in the first few years, the appeals became increasingly forceful. Parents were told they could be responsible for the death of their child if they did not accept the help of the KLV. In some jurisdictions, like the Rhine-Ruhr region, parents were required to sign statements declaring that they had been repeatedly made aware of the dangers to which they exposed their children by leaving them behind in air-raid emergency areas, but had nevertheless refused to accept the assistance offered by the Party and the State, and that they therefore expressly took full responsibility for the loss of their children's health or life as a result of future enemy air raids.

By 1943, entire classrooms were ordered to evacuate the regions identified as air-war zones, and school instruction was suspended in those areas. Any children staying behind would no longer receive schooling, placing parents in violation of the education laws, in effect forcing them to send their children to the KLV and ending all pretence of the scheme being voluntary.

Part II

The Führer Takes Care of Our Children

Chapter 9

Konstanz

The bombing had become so heavy by 1943 that it became obvious normal school instruction was not going to be possible anymore. Witten had almost miraculously escaped the worst so far, but neighbouring cities had been devastated. In Wuppertal the asphalt had boiled, and Bochum's city centre had been levelled, as had Cologne's and Düsseldorf's, claiming many thousands of civilian casualties. It was inevitable that the children of Witten would have to be evacuated soon under the auspices of the KLV, the children's relocation programme. My parents were suspicious of this programme that was going to take their child away, even though it was meant to protect me. Despite the government's assurances that the kids would be perfectly safe, they were deeply uneasy and worried about what would happen to me in a place where they could not reach me.

Eventually, we got the word. The children of Witten were to depart between 14 and 21 July 1943.

* * *

The long dark train, half freight, half passenger, was waiting for us at Witten station on the morning of 20 July. It was going to take us, 260 students of the Witten School for Boys plus 160 mothers and siblings, away from our homes to the faraway city of Konstanz, a long way south near the Swiss border, where we were told we would be safe. But nobody knew how long we would be gone.

The station was dirty and noisy. Loudspeakers were announcing imminent departures I couldn't make out. The coal dust from the depot next door covered everything in a sooty film, the pipes from the natural gas installations were sticking up into the sky. It was hot, and the air smelled of burnt coal.

Our class had shrunk already, because some parents had taken their kids out of school to the countryside to bypass the evacuation. There were only twenty left of my class of forty seventh-graders. Some of my friends were gone, I didn't know where. The platform was crowded with parents and suitcases, bags, carts and boxes of all sizes, and kids were running everywhere. Everybody was shoving and pushing to climb on the train, and I was struggling to get on to the steep step up to the carriage with my suitcase in tow. Somebody grabbed me by my arms and heaved me in.

Mama and Papa had come to see me off. Mama said she would follow soon and stay with me for a while. She was wearing her Sunday hat with a big flower on the side, and her church gloves, and Papa was sporting his Sunday best, too. As I was pulled on to the train I turned around to look for them on the platform, but they were not in the spot where they were supposed to be. I tried to focus, to make out their faces in the crowd, but I couldn't find them.

Where are they? My heart started beating a little faster. Scanning the sea of faces, I couldn't make them out. My palms became sweaty.

'Mama! Papa!' I yelled over the crowd.

The whistle blew. It was the signal that the train was about to leave the station. I swallowed. I wanted to get off.

'Mama! Papa!'

My eyes started welling up with tears, and sweat trickled down my back. I didn't know what to do. This wasn't supposed to be happening. I was supposed to be able to say goodbye to them. I felt like I should jump out of the train; I was ready to bolt. My eyes darted everywhere, my heart was thumping. Suddenly I spotted my father's hat amid the ocean of heads. Instantly my fists unclenched; I had not even realized they were balled up. He had seen me, too.

'Papa, Papa, where is Mama?' I yelled, cupping my hands around my mouth to amplify the sound.

'She's right here,' he shouted over the din, pointing to his left.

Maybe I had not looked that way before. I saw her hat materialize in the crowd. Another whistle, a slight jolt, the feeling that the platform was moving. But it was I who was moving; the train was leaving the station.

'Papa! Mama! Bye-bye!' I shouted, willing my voice to reach them.

Papa was walking fast, trying to keep up with the accelerating train as we waved to each other. Mama started falling back. My guts tightened as I saw my parents' figures shrinking, getting left behind. I waved until I couldn't make them out anymore.

Restless, I turned left and walked down the compartment to find a place to sit. Everything was changing, and my stomach was tied in knots, aching for my parents.

But somehow, strangely, it was exciting, too. It was an adventure. The famous Lake Konstanz was waiting for us at our destination, and it was supposed to be beautiful. Before we left they had shown us our new 'war home', the historic city of Konstanz, on pretty, colourful postcards and brochures. Although they were sending our teachers with us to ensure our instruction continued while away in Konstanz – those teachers that were left, that is, the old men, the young women and the men who had something wrong with them – we believed it was all going to be like a big field trip.

* * *

Konstanz was far away, and the ride was long and slow. We had to stop constantly to allow military convoys to pass, and lots of detours were necessary because so much track had been destroyed by Allied bombing. The train was old, powered by a steam locomotive. Those of us who found a seat were crowded twelve or more in compartments meant to seat six. The kids unlucky enough not to have managed to find a place to sit had to stand in the narrow corridor or sit on their suitcases, flattening themselves against the side every time somebody walked through. In the compartment our overflowing luggage was precariously stowed overhead, threatening to tumble down at every jolt of the train. We sat on wooden benches that faced each other. A pull-down window was on one side, and on the other was a scratched and damaged sliding door with a metal latch that did not work. The constant clatter and shake of the train on the tracks had a hypnotic effect on me, and I eventually dozed off into a dreamless slumber.

It was night when the train arrived in Konstanz. The platform was noisy and crowded with the host families, who had been waiting for us kids for some time. We were herded out on to the platform wearing around our necks the tags that had been passed out to us before we had boarded the train in Witten. The tags had written on them our names and the names of the host family we had been assigned to. There was a great commotion and a lot of pushing and shoving, while the teachers and the government handlers who had come along to keep an eye on everything were trying to get us lined up in some kind of order to pair us up with our host families. That exercise seemed to take forever, and I was tired and hungry. Our names were called in alphabetical order. When they called your name, you yelled 'Present' and stepped forward. Then the name of the host family was called, and hopefully the family was there to retrieve you.

What if nobody shows up to get you? Do they send you back home, or do they just leave you here? I was cold, clammy and tired, sitting on my luggage, waiting for my name to be called, worrying about what would happen to me if nobody came. Although I was surrounded by a big crowd of people, I had never felt so alone in my life.

I looked around to distract myself. The line behind me was quite long. Suddenly I felt sorry for the poor devils whose surname was at the end of the alphabet, like my friend Helmut Von Rathenau. *Boy, he has a long way to go.*

My name was called and I automatically shot up. I was to stay with a family whose name was Vollmar. A pang of nerves shot through me. Suddenly my knees went a little weak and my palms started sweating. I was about to be led away by some total stranger to a place I did not know. I did not want to be there, but having no other choice, I slowly took a step forward. Frau Vollmar stepped out to meet me. She was a pleasant-looking middle-aged lady of medium build, with wavy, dark brown hair. She wore a plaid jacket and matching plaid skirt, and sturdy-looking brown shoes.

'*Grüss Gott*, Willi,' she said energetically, using the typical South German and Swiss greeting, which translates as 'God's greetings', instead of the common '*Heil Hitler*' salute.

My heartbeat slowed a little.

'*Grüss Gott*, Frau Vollmar,' I quickly replied, bowing my head respectfully, relieved that she looked motherly and nice.

'Welcome to Konstanz, Willi. Follow me.'

I complied, following her quick, decisive steps through the packed platform to the exit.

'Did you have a pleasant trip?'

'Yes, Frau Vollmar.'

'Are you hungry?'

I hesitated. 'Yes, Frau Vollmar,' I said in a small voice.

'Willi, what is your middle name?'

'Johannes, Frau Vollmar.'

'Ah, good, Hans …'

This was the abbreviation of Johannes and a very popular German boy's name.

'Well, you see, our eldest son's name is also Willi, and that could turn into a bit of a problem. So in order to avoid any confusion from the start, what we are going to do is this: we are going to call you Hans Willi. That is a nice name, isn't it?'

Confused, I nodded weakly. 'Yes, Frau Vollmar.'

'Well, that's settled then, Hans Willi. Off we go.'

My name had just been changed, but I was too stunned and shy to protest. Speechless, I followed her to what was to become my new home.

Chapter 10

The Vollmars

The Vollmar family lived in the Peterhausen district, on 30 Spanierstrasse. Their apartment was on the fifth floor and it had a balcony with a view of the mountains. It was not large, which made for cramped quarters, as the Vollmar family had eight children, five of whom were boys. There were always quarrels about access to the bathroom in the morning. Somehow the girls always managed to slip in first and take the longest, while we boys stood in line in our underwear jumping from one foot to the other in urgent need of the toilet, protesting loudly. 'Come on already, what are you doing in there?' was the usual complaint, typically met with stony silence or a giggle from the other side of the door. Except for the two youngest boys, who slept in Frau Vollmar's bedroom, we all slept in one bedroom with two beds in it, one for the girls and one for the boys. That meant there were four of us in one bed, and I permanently had somebody's feet in my face.

My mother soon followed on a special train to Konstanz to be close to me. She had to stay in a hotel in town, as there was no space for her at the Vollmars' overcrowded apartment, but she was so happy to see me she didn't seem to mind too much. I would often stay with her overnight to keep her company. After class, I would do my homework in the hotel room, and as I worked, she would go through the routine of unwrapping the many smoked and dried sausages she had brought in her suitcase and spreading them out on the table to prepare a snack.

'Tante Änne packed us some nice sausages,' she nodded to herself as she cut off thick savoury slices of *Mettwurst* and *Dauerwurst* for the two of us.

She had a seemingly endless supply, having entirely filled a small suitcase with the stuff. I was thoroughly enjoying these rare meals from the farm back home, given that food was anything but plentiful at the Vollmars. I knew Mama had to call in a few favours from the cousins to get a hold of these precious supplies.

'Here, you take a couple of these to Frau Vollmar,' she added, rolling a few large specimens up in extra paper and setting them aside on the table.

'*Ach*, and Onkel Konrad's dachshund had a litter of eight puppies, can you believe it?'

I smiled. 'Can we get one, Mama?'

'No, you know how Papa is about animals in the house, but you'll be able to go and see them at Onkel Konrad's soon.'

I nodded, hoping I would soon be back at home playing with my cousins and the puppies.

We went on walks around town and explored its many historical sites, which we both enjoyed. But eventually we knew that our time was ending. My mother could not stay for ever in a hotel; she was spending all the little money she had and she couldn't put her life on hold indefinitely. She had to face reality and return to Witten.

I told her, 'Mama, don't leave Papa so alone. There is war in the Ruhr Valley and all, and he needs your support.'

'*Ach*, Willi, I know, I know, but I can't leave you. You are only thirteen.'

'I'll be all right, Mama. The Vollmars are nice people. I am not alone like Papa.'

I told her this because I felt that I had to grow up and be a man. As the Führer said, 'German boys are … tough as leather, swift as greyhounds and hard as Krupp steel'. Also, because I didn't want my schoolmates to think I was a weakling who had to have his mummy around, although that was exactly what I wanted. My heart ached when she left, but I pretended it was no big deal, although I didn't fool Frau Vollmar for a minute. I caught her looking at me a few times when I thought I was alone. I knew she could see my sadness.

* * *

Frau Vollmar was Swiss. She had married a German who was not a member of the Nazi party but employed by a company called Todt. This was a paramilitary organization which built protective walls around Germany, like the famous *Westwall* on the German-French border, also known as the Siegfried Line. Frau Vollmar had been expelled from Switzerland because she was married to a German. Switzerland was neutral and made a show of wanting nothing to do with Germany, although Swiss bankers had no qualms about accepting Reichsmarks and German gold into their vaults.

Herr Vollmar was never there, since he was always deployed somewhere else building his walls. I only saw him twice in the year and a half I lived with the family. Frau Vollmar had to cope on her own. Taking me in was not voluntary, of course; families were compelled to take on KLV children. Many families resented their unwanted guests, and host families' children would often be mean to us outsiders from faraway towns who ended up being a nuisance to them, nothing more than another mouth to feed. I was lucky that the Vollmars always treated me like one of their own. They understood how badly I missed my parents.

Frau Vollmar's sister, who did not have children of her own, lived with the family to help with the household. Frau Vollmar took in sewing jobs for other people to make ends meet, in addition to sewing the clothes for all her children, so she barely had time for anything else. Food and fuel had to be procured, however, and that meant standing in long queues with ration cards in hand. There were different-coloured coupons for monthly allocations of meat, bread, milk, soap, fabric, firewood for the kitchen stove and for the *Kachelofen*, the one and only heating stove which weakly radiated just enough heat to keep us from freezing in winter, and for every other necessary item. People usually ran out of ration stamps before the month ended, so that the last week of each month was always especially tough. I thought of my parents often, wondering if they were hungry and cold too, aching to be with them.

The food was being rationed in all cities, even here, and the Vollmars had nine mouths to feed. So in the evenings we ate *Mehlsuppe*, flour soup. This poor man's dish consisted of flour sprinkled on to a pan, with no fat, then browned. To this browned flour you added water, and what resulted was the soup. Because nobody could get a full belly from eating that, we were all quite thin. I never felt full in the years I was in Konstanz, and not until a long time after the war ended.

* * *

Since the entire school of Witten had been relocated to Konstanz, and our teachers had come along too, we continued our lessons, though with a reduced selection of subjects, since all the able-bodied male teachers had been sent to the front. We shared the school with the children of Konstanz. They were taught in the morning, and we had our classes in the afternoon.

One day in a History lesson my classmates and I decided to annoy the teachers. We had got hold of film negatives which, when set on fire, smelled terrible. We called them stink bombs and we decided to release them in Dr Sternkopf's history class. But it turned out that when Dr Sternkopf had been a soldier in the First World War he had been *verschüttet*, buried in debris, as a consequence of which he had lost all sense of smell. The stench of the negatives had no effect whatsoever on Dr Sternkopf, whom we also called '*Doktor Ecke*' (Dr Corner), on account of his sharpness.

He couldn't smell the negatives we had set on fire, but we could, and our eyes were watering from the stench, so we politely asked him, '*Herr Doktor*, can we open the windows?'

It was very cold outside, and he said, 'Children, be careful. Many people have frozen to death, but nobody has ever been stunk to death.'

Then we realized – he had worked out what we were up to!

My classmates and I were country bumpkins. We came from the Ruhr valley, the coal and steel belt of Germany, and here we were, transported to the medieval city of Konstanz and its famous lake, with its beautiful marketplace and historic buildings. It was a fantastic experience for us, kids from a medium-sized, rather unattractive industrial town with little history, to be exposed to all this art and culture. There were steamboats on the lake; unlike modern boats powered by liquid fuel, these were old rust-buckets that still ran on coal, but to us they looked grand. They had big paddle-wheels that ploughed through the water and slowly propelled them across the lake. I marvelled at how regal they looked.

Across from Konstanz on the other side of the lake were the towns of Meersburg and Unterhuldingen. They used to take us there often on excursions. Meersburg was a romantic old medieval town with a fortress, excellent for walks on sleepy afternoons, but the neighbouring town of Unterhuldingen was especially interesting. They had reconstructed some ancient Germanic dwellings there, a so-called 'water settlement' or village on stilts in the lake. One day, we were taken there on an educational field trip. We crossed a planked walkway from the shore to a small wooden house sitting on posts planted in the water. There were ancient artefacts in the kitchen, goblets and plates from which the original dwellers had drunk and eaten so long ago, and bowls and other utensils I could not readily recognize. It was the first time in my life that I had seen anything like that, and it amazed me. I stood in the middle of the kitchen staring at the worn old wooden implements and imagined men clad in animal skins with long, braided beards, and barefoot women in long, heavy skirts filling their goblets with ale. The teacher's voice woke me from my daydream.

'Willi, *komm schon*, let's go. We have to leave.'

The magical images that ancient village had conjured up in my mind stayed with me. I began to realize the world was much bigger than I had ever imagined and started wondering what else there was to see out there.

About two kilometres from Unterhuldingen was the city of Friedrichshafen. This was a famous city known, long before the Führer came to power, as the place where Graf Zeppelin had built his airship. The old Zeppelin factory still stood, but in the Third Reich other things were built there – weapons, the devil knew what kind. I watched from Konstanz as the Allied air forces bombed this factory. It was the same air show I had witnessed in Witten and in Dortmund, beautiful to look at, but by then I knew that many people had lost their lives in raids.

Another town on the lake was Bregenz. This was Austrian territory, but Austria was now part of Greater Germany, so we could go there without needing a passport. One day, we went on a field trip to the city, and the border patrol gave us funny looks because we were in our *Hitlerjugend* uniforms. We elbowed each other and giggled, exchanging knowing looks, showing the pride that we had been taught and believing ourselves part of an elite. We had been told this over and over; it was on the cover of our school reading book in the words of the Führer himself: 'Because you, my boys, you are the living guarantors of Germany, you are the living Germany of the future.'

* * *

At some point that year I received my first suit with long trousers. This was a big deal because it was a rite of passage, the sign that I was becoming a young man. Up to that point I had worn only shorts, either the *Jungvolk* uniform or lederhosen. My parents had the suit tailored and sent to Konstanz. As Frau Vollmar took it out of the box and smoothed out the wrinkles, I marvelled at it and wondered how expensive it must have been to have such a smart suit especially made just for me. My chest felt tight as I thought of Mama and Papa not being able to share this milestone with me.

Frau Vollmar glanced at me and said, 'Hans Willi, let's take a nice picture of you in your suit to send to your parents.'

I swallowed hard and nodded.

She took a picture of me standing on her balcony so Mama and Papa could at least have an image of the special moment they were missing. I saw the photo before she posted it off. It showed a thirteen-year-old kid with a goofy grin on his face looking out at the world with wonder. In the background was the majestic Swiss mountain known as the Säntis, which could be seen clearly from the Vollmars' balcony. Every time I looked at that mountain I wanted to explore what lay beyond. I daydreamed about unknown, exciting places I had read or heard about and decided I would travel all over the world when I grew up.

* * *

'Willi, do you want to make a little money?' said a brother-in-law of Frau Vollmar, the costume manager of the Konstanz Stadttheater theatre, when he stopped by the apartment one day.

'Oh, yes, sir,' I replied eagerly.

I was definitely keen, as we never got enough to eat, and extra money meant I could buy some *Brötchen*, small rolls of white bread, in town. It turned out they needed some tall 'extras' at the theatre, and I seemed to fit the bill because I was taller than average. I signed up right away and I was to earn 50 Reichsmarks for every performance. The job was easy; it consisted of putting on a costume, walking up on the stage and standing in the background. Nothing to it.

The trouble was that I had a big head. My parents always had problems finding headgear for me, as my hat size was a 60, and 60 was, well, extra-large. My role at the theatre was to play a soldier who was a prison guard in Beethoven's opera *Fidelio*, and the soldier wore a helmet.

The evening of the first performance arrived. The show started, and it was my time to go on stage. While the crew had instructed me what to do, they had unfortunately neglected to conduct a wardrobe rehearsal. When the time came and they tried to put the helmet on my head, it was too small. It sat perched on top of my head with no hope of making it down over my crown.

'Oh, *Scheisse*, what do we do?' they looked at each other, panicking slightly.

'Wait, what's wrong?' I asked, not sure I liked the look in their eyes.

'Hold on tight, Willi, we're going to have to get this thing to go over your head one way or another.'

They pulled the helmet down really hard and over my eyes, so that I couldn't see a thing. It then got stuck and wouldn't budge.

'Wait. I can't see,' I protested, but to no avail.

'Hush, you'll be all right, just march straight in front of you, about six steps, and then stop, got it? GO!'

I received a decisive nudge that propelled me forward, so that retreat was no longer an option. As I stumbled on to the stage with as much dignity as I could muster, the audience started to laugh, even though it was a tragic piece. It became abundantly clear that wardrobe had to look for a new helmet.

I ended up appearing in fifty *Fidelio* performances altogether and earned at total of 1,500 Reichsmarks, which I invested entirely in food. Every time I got paid, I would run to the bakery on my way home and get two warm, fragrant *Brötchen* that had just come out of the oven, then wolfed them down as I walked, eating so fast that sometimes I would choke. There was never so much as a crumb left by the time I got to the house.

At the conclusion of the fiftieth performance I received a certificate of recognition that confirmed my loyal participation. I beamed when I received it because I had earned it with my own work. I knew Papa would be proud of me and I just couldn't wait to show him. But my father never got to see it. That certificate I held so dear would be, like everything else, destroyed in the war.

Chapter 11

Christmas 1943

Christmas was approaching. Since my father worked for the Reichsbahn he had access to train tickets, and one day Frau Vollmar received a letter from him with a free return ticket from Konstanz to Witten for me. The big question was, how was the travel from Konstanz to Witten going to work? I was with the *Jungvolk* and I was also part of the KLV. We were monitored so we would not get into any mischief, and we were not allowed to go home. It didn't matter that I had a ticket; the *Hitlerjugend* guards who patrolled the station were not going to let me get on the train. My parents obviously did not realize this. Disobeying the authorities could spell a lot of trouble for all of us. I could be disciplined and taken away to somewhere a lot less pleasant, where I might have to do physical labour. My host family would probably be punished for not being able to control me and suffer a consequence like losing food stamps. But knowing how I longed to see my parents, the Vollmars decided to help me.

We arrived at the station close to the time my train was to depart but we did not go inside. The station was bustling with people, either leaving or arriving to be reunited with their families in anticipation of Christmas. Military police, the *Feldgendarmerie*, were on patrol. We could also see the *Hitlerjugend* guards who were there to make sure that no *Hitlerjugend* or *Jungvolk* kids could sneak through without proper authorization. They walked up and down the crowded platforms in their smart brown shirts with the swastika on their left arm, their field knives on their black leather belts. There was no way I could get on directly from the platform;

the guards were everywhere. To get on unnoticed I would have to go to the rear of the train.

We walked along the outside perimeter until we got to where we could see the tracks extending into the distance. The train I wanted to board was there. As long as the guards didn't look my way, I would be all right. You could get to the tracks quite easily; there were no barriers blocking access. Frau Vollmar's two eldest sons were my lookouts; they would watch out for police and *Hitlerjugend* so I could run over the tracks to get to the train. We walked along a street that ran parallel to the tracks, a waist-high wall separating the two.

'Everybody keep walking and don't look around you. Look ahead,' Frau Vollmar reminded us.

We complied. She did not want us to slow down too much or hesitate, lest we attracted unwanted attention, but luckily the street was empty. The Vollmars fell back a little, and I kept walking ahead until we arrived at the end of the train, where the low wall also happened to end. I walked just past it, slowing my pace to a stroll. Frau Vollmar kept going at a brisk pace as if on her way to an appointment. She was to meet up with the boys later, on the other side of the station. The Vollmar boys slowed down, cleared the wall and turned left off the street toward the tracks. They leaned against the wall and waited for an opportunity when the guards were not looking our way. Once they gave the 'all clear' hand signal – a sharp up and down movement of the forearm – I was to run on to the tracks and jump on the last carriage of the train. I had to cross two sets of tracks to get to the train and I had to be fast. The guards could turn to look at any moment. My eyes were fixed on the Vollmar boys.

The signal came immediately, and I just ran. There could have been a train coming from the other way, but I didn't care. Nothing was going to keep me from getting home.

Don't look … Blood was pulsing in my ears. The distance was narrowing in front of me as I flew across the tracks, my legs propelling me forward as if of their own will. Fire raged in my chest. *A few more yards … yes …* I clambered on to the train. That is when I exhaled. I was on my way home.

Nobody seemed to have taken any notice of me. Now I had to find a place to hide. I started walking past the compartments, still breathing heavily, not sure what I was looking for or how to avoid the guards who patrolled the inside of the trains. I spotted a couple of older peasant women sitting by themselves who looked friendly and decided to take a chance.

'*Entschuldigung* (excuse me),' I said to them as I opened the compartment door, interrupting their conversation.

They looked up at me with surprise.

'What is it, *Junge*?'

'I'm on my way to Witten to see my parents but I'm not supposed to be, and if the guards find me, I'll get in trouble and they'll send me back. Can you help me hide?'

'*Junge*, don't worry, we'll get you home.'

They smiled and waved me in. I think it was like a challenge for them. They looked almost excited to be able to play a trick on the guards.

The *Feldgendarmerie* and the *Hitlerjugend* came by often during the trip to check on the passengers. The women's strategy was to hide me under their long, multilayered skirts, since nobody would ever dream of looking there. It was stuffy – and smelly – under those skirts, but I didn't complain. When the coast was clear, they would tell me, and I would come up for air for a while.

During the trip, the train was attacked by Allied aircraft. We heard the heavy drone of the planes in the distance over the dull clatter of the train on the tracks, rapidly becoming louder and higher-pitched. There were several. They were going to shoot at us.

'Quick, on the ground away from the window! Cover your head!' urged the women.

I crouched on the floor, arms over my head. They just sat where they were, heads bowed and eyes closed, hands clasped in prayer. Luckily, the aim of these pilots was not good, and a lot of their machine-gun fire went rattling past us, leaving a trail of holes and dust in the fields as the train kept moving. We heard a few startled cries and the scuffle of feet, but most people made little noise. There wasn't a lot of commotion because people were resigned to the fact there was nothing anybody could do about it, so we just remained quiet and hoped to survive. A few shots struck the roof, but none of the bullets penetrated it.

'Thank God they didn't drop any bombs …' sighed one of the peasant women, fingering the beads of the rosary she had been holding tight in her hand.

'Amen,' nodded the other woman. 'Amen, praised be the Lord.'

I finally arrived in Witten, feeling lucky. I had made it, and maybe things would turn out all right after all. Mama and Papa were overjoyed. The Christmas tree was in the living room, brightly lit with candles clipped on to its branches. My mother baked biscuits with the rationed butter and flour she was able to find, and their aroma permeated the house, reminding me of all the happy Christmases that had come before. All four candles were lit on the Advent wreath on the dining room table. Christmas carols were sung, and we visited relatives. On Christmas Eve my parents had a present for me. It was an air rifle. Its barrel was made of polished, shiny metal, smooth to the touch. I stroked the rifle with pride of ownership swelling in my chest and took it outside to try out as soon as I had a chance. I shot at some squirrels and birds out in the back garden, but they were too fast, and I didn't hit any. The fun was not so much in hitting the mark as in playing with a gun that belonged to me. I had never had something so valuable before.

This was all I wanted. I was home with my parents and never wanted to leave again. It was as if for a brief interval time stood still and everything was all right. But the inescapable reality soon set in that I had to return to Konstanz before trouble followed me home.

In early January I boarded the train in Witten. I didn't have to sneak on this time. Because my father was a senior employee of the Reichsbahn, I just went with him and he got me on, although that was all he could do for me.

'Willi, take care. If you explain why you are travelling alone, they will understand.'

'OK, Papa, I will.'

It was awkward. I was not telling my dad what I expected was going to happen. Instead, I agreed with him that I could just 'explain' something to the *Feldgendarmerie* or the *Hitlerjugend* guards, knowing all the while there was no explanation that would get me out of this mess without consequences. I hadn't exactly told my parents what happened on my way to Witten, so Papa still believed that I could travel as long as I had a valid ticket. I hadn't the heart to correct his belief that the only complication that could arise was the fact that I was a minor travelling alone. But the problem wasn't that I was travelling unaccompanied – it was that I was travelling at all. Papa, meanwhile, seemed to firmly believe in the common sense and reasonable nature of the authorities, who would surely see the logic in my arguments for travelling alone. It was disconcerting to me that I knew better. I had broken the rules and therefore I would inevitably be punished. But I didn't want to worry him, and it wasn't my place to correct him, so I kept quiet.

Once on the train, I was on my own.

There was no lack of farm folk travelling on the train, often with livestock, typically chickens or ducks in cages. As they didn't seem to be scrutinized too carefully by the guards, and they had helped me on the way to Witten, I went looking for farmers, hoping for the best. I was actually lucky enough to find another set of peasant women who were willing to hide me under their long skirts until I arrived in Konstanz. The compartment was occupied by four women. They were friendly and talkative and asked me questions about my family. Maybe they thought of their own sons when they saw me and that is why they helped me. Maybe their sons were fighting at the front. How many husbands, brothers, sons had they lost? They couldn't protect them, far out of their reach as they were, but perhaps they thought they could help me in a small way, and that brought them some comfort.

As I sat under the voluminous skirts once more, hiding from the guards, I started thinking about the women's sons, the brave soldiers who were risking their life to defend our country. They were heroes to me. They were keeping us safe from our enemies who wanted to kill us. I wanted to be brave like them.

The *HJ* guards and the *Feldgendarmerie*, carrying guns, were waiting on the platform as the train pulled up in Konstanz. I peeked out of the window as it came to a halt and saw the officers checking every passenger's credentials. There was no way I was getting off the train unnoticed.

'You, your name?' a *Feldgendarmerie* police officer, flanked by two *HJ* guards asked me as soon as I stepped out.

'Langbein,' I managed to reply, sweating profusely despite the bitter winter cold.

He glanced at a list in his hands, then nodded at the *HJ* guards. I froze. They grabbed me, handcuffed me and started walking, pushing me in front of them.

'*Los, marsch!*' (hurry up, march), barked the officer, poking me in the back with his gun. I tripped over my own feet because my knees had turned to pudding.

'*Komm schon, lauf schneller*' (come on, walk faster), one of the *HJ* guards said sharply, hurrying me to the end of the platform along the wall of the building that spanned the entire length of the station. My head was screaming *run* as I stumbled along, my eyes darting around, hoping to catch the attention of someone who could help me. Nobody was looking my way. It was as if I were invisible.

'HALT!' came the sudden command.

They opened a nondescript door and shoved me into what looked like an empty storage room somewhere in the back of the station. I was terrified. My throat had closed, I could not utter a single sound. They pushed me down hard into a little chair in the middle of the empty room and stood around me, looking very unfriendly. They started interrogating me.

'What did you do in Witten? Who did you talk to there?'

'My parents,' I squeaked.

'Do you think we are fools? What were you really doing there?' Their voices rose.

'It's true, I swear.'

I blurted out that my father was in the Party, and all kinds of other things.

'I don't want to live with the Vollmar family, I want to be back with my parents. They relocated me there with the KLV, I don't belong in Konstanz.'

They had to know that, but they just looked at each other sceptically.

'How did you get on the train? Don't you know it is forbidden for you to leave your host family? Is that how you show obedience to the Führer? You're a liar and a cheat, why should we believe anything you say?'

One of the interrogators fired off questions in a rapid crescendo, getting closer and closer to my face.

'I didn't do anything wrong. I was just homesick. I am not a spy, I swear,' I pleaded, along with anything else I could think of saying to get me out of that pickle.

Abruptly, without a word, they turned and left the room, locking the door behind them and leaving me alone in there. I was panting. I had no idea what was going to happen next. Every minute seemed like an eternity.

What are they going to do to me? What if they don't let me go? I just want to go home. I needed to pee, I was cold, the circulation in my hands was getting cut off and my fingers were going numb. I started crying softly, which made the situation worse, because I couldn't wipe the snot off my nose.

Eventually, after what seemed forever to me, they came back. I vainly tried to read the expression on their faces.

'The *Hitlerjugend* Command has decided to let you go with only a light punishment this time,' said one *HJ* guard standing in front of me in a wide-legged stance, his arms folded in front of him, while the other one undid my handcuffs. The *Feldgendarme* was not with them.

I breathed out, slightly encouraged by his words. I shook my hands, trying to restore circulation.

'As your punishment, you will clean the toilets at this station for the next fourteen days. You are to report to the Stationmaster at 6.30 am tomorrow morning for your cleaning instructions. You can see yourself out now,' the HJ guard said with a wolfish grin.

My mouth gaped open. I heard a muffled guffaw coming from the other guard.

'Heil Hitler!' they commanded.

I shot out of my seat. 'Heil Hitler!' I croaked.

They clicked their heels and turned to leave. I saw them elbowing each other on their way out. My shoulders slumped. I knew then that I was going to be the source of considerable amusement to the *HJ* organization for the next couple of weeks. They were going to have a good laugh at my expense, and there was nothing I could do about it, much as I hated being the butt of their jokes. All things considered, I pondered as I walked out of the station, it had all been worth it to see my parents. I would still have done it even if I had known beforehand what the punishment was going to be.

The other thing I knew now was that it was no use trying to make myself scarce. There was no getting away. I was back with the Vollmar family for good.

Chapter 12

The Hitler Youth

I graduated from the *Jungvolk* into the *Hitlerjugend* when I turned fourteen in May 1944. As disciplined as the *Jungvolk* had been, starting with a flag salute every morning, followed by marching drills, listening to recitations of the Führer's doctrine and singing of patriotic songs before school every day, the *HJ* was a more practical organization. It was subdivided into various groups, each of which would lead to a military specialization. For instance, there was a group for future pilots, the *Segelflieger* (glider pilots), which was called the *Flieger-HJ*, and other groups for infantry and naval disciplines. I was placed in a group that was under the purview of the NSKK, the *National Sozialistische Kraftfahrer Kur*, the National Socialist Motorized Unit. We were to learn to ride motorcycles and were supposed to receive both theoretical and practical instruction. Unfortunately, there were no motorcycles to be ridden because the military had requisitioned them all, and our unit leader, who was easygoing, used to say, 'Boys, do what you want. Take off,' and we would run off and play for a while.

As spotty as the *HJ* paramilitary instruction turned out to be, school life was even more inconsistent. A few weeks after our initial arrival at Konstanz in the summer of 1943, the mayor of Allensbach, a neighbouring town, had contacted our headmaster, Herr Noelle, with the following request:

21 Sept. 1943
As next week marks the beginning of the potato, fruit and grape harvest, I would like to ask that you request of the appropriate authority to grant the young boys lodged here a 14-day leave period so that they can be employed in harvest duties.
       Heil Hitler

The mayor's request was supported by a 1942 decree which held that the securing of food was the most important duty of the German people next to military service, and thus the German youth had to make itself available for that effort. According to the decree, 'The war engagement counts as fulfillment of school duties.'

The extent to which the decree cared about our school education and our future career prospects was pretty obvious. More and more demands came for us to be pulled out of school and work in the fields. In the second half of 1944 we enjoyed just fourteen days of school in one entire term. Not that we cared. We thought it was great to miss school.

Chapter 13

Military Training

In early September 1944 three Waffen-SS Panzer troop commanders came to our school looking for soldiers.

'Boys, a great privilege is being bestowed on you today by the Führer.'

They stood in front of the class, impressive in their double-breasted black uniforms with the SS-runes on their high collars, black breeches and slick black leather boots, the German eagle and swastika prominent on their officers' hats.

'Today, we are going to select a few of you to receive valuable military training so that you can defend our Fatherland against the Bolshevik threat, the enemies of the Reich who want to destroy us.'

We listened in awe. It was a great honour to be chosen to defend our country, and it made us proud. My mind replayed the newsreels that reported on the evil Allied forces that wanted to finish us, first by bombing all our cities to kill all civilians, then by torturing and starving the survivors, and the heroic efforts our soldiers were making to protect our mothers and fathers, brothers and sisters. The German troops were pushing the enemy back, and we were going to prevail. Our teachers and our schoolbooks told us that we were Germany's hope and its future, that we were superior and we would win.

The Führer had issued the *Volkssturm* (Home Guard) decree, drafting all men between the ages of sixteen and sixty because he was running out of soldiers. The Nazis started by conscripting the old men who were no longer fit for war and those with minor disabilities who had previously been rejected for duty. Anybody who could hold a gun was sent off to the front to fight the 'total war', the effort to engage every resource of Germany into the war effort above any other priority.

We were next. Children were being drafted to fill the void left by the fallen, the losses at the front having become too heavy. This was a pattern repeating itself from the First World War. In 1917 schools had been put into the service of the war effort, leading to the creation of *Schülerwehrkompanien*, Student Military Battalions. Children from our very school had been given military training, deployed to the factories to manufacture ammunition and sent to the fields to help with the harvest. We were the unwitting participants in a repeat performance.

We had been sent to Konstanz to stay with host families to protect us from the heavy Allied bombing in our home towns. But here was Hitler's elite paramilitary corps calling us to action.

Two of the officers walked down the middle aisle between our desks in silence, scrutinizing us carefully, while the third one stayed at the front. The only sounds in the room were their heavy footsteps as they paced slowly up and down.

Eventually, they made their choice. They went to stand in front again and pointed.

'You, you and you, come and stand with us.'

They picked out three of us because we were obviously the biggest and strongest. It didn't seem to matter to them that we were only fourteen years old.

When I saw the finger pointing in my direction, my mind went back to the day I travelled as a stowaway on the train to spend Christmas with my parents. I remembered the peasant women whose sons were at the front, fighting for us. I had wished then that I could be brave like them. Here was my chance. It was scary, but it also sounded like an exciting adventure. The three of us would defend our country and make the Führer proud. We would march into battle and defeat the enemy or die. We were going to wear smart uniforms, ride mighty tanks and carry powerful weapons that would strike fear into the hearts of the enemy. I stood up and looked at the other two kids.

We could not show any apprehension or nervousness lest we look like cowards, so we puffed out our chests, acting big, and walked to the front. The other boys looked at us with wonder, some of them jealous that they hadn't been selected.

'What makes him so special?' I heard one kid say later in the hallway.

'Don't know, but I do know you didn't get picked, you loser,' I sniggered as I passed, feeling smug.

We were sent to a *Wehrertüchtigungslager*, a military training camp, in Trauenstein, a town south of Munich near the majestic Chiemsee lake. It was a two-month programme intended to teach us how to handle several different weapons. After the training, we were to return to school and resume our normal activities but would be called if the Führer needed us. Among the weapons we were taught to use was the Walther P-38 pistol and the *Sturmgewehr* machine gun. We were told that this was the first machine gun in the world that was accurate at 1,000m, a superior piece of equipment. The last thing they taught us to fire was the *Panzerfaust*, the anti-tank rocket launcher, a weapon designed to blow up enemy tanks. They explained to us that German weapons were more advanced than and far superior to the armament of our enemies, especially the Bolsheviks, who sometimes still used primitive horse-drawn carriages. We were told that not only was our weaponry superior but also our intellect.

The course lasted from early September to the end of October 1944. We were quickly disabused of the notion that this was in any way a glamorous assignment, as we had somehow imagined when we were picked out for the privilege. The barracks where we stayed were large two-storey buildings, with mess halls and offices on the ground floor and dormitories upstairs. We got up at 6 o'clock in the morning, were given little to eat then and not much more for the rest of the day. There were non-stop drills from dawn until sunset. At night, utterly exhausted and with grumbling stomachs, we crawled up the stairs by the skin of our teeth to the dorms, and the whole thing started again at six in the morning the next day. We did get to watch a lot of newsreels. On the movie screen the German eagle would spread its wings to the sound of fanfares, and we listened to the triumphant updates of how German troops had won back territory from the enemy. The German soldier was invincible, and our instructors told us we were to become national heroes. We looked at each other with a sense of pride, knowing we were going to do something important. After all, what could be more important than defending your country?

Only much later would I find out that at that point Germany was in retreat on every front, sustaining heavy casualties in a war that had already been lost.

Chapter 14

Schleching

Our days in the idyllic town of Konstanz were numbered. The war situation was deteriorating. Streams of bedraggled refugees from the east came flooding into the city in October and filled the schools, the gyms, all public places. Reports of the atrocities committed by the Russian army had provoked a huge wave of people to leave the eastern part of the Reich. Millions were fleeing to western Germany, telling terrifying stories about the Red Army literally rolling over the columns of refugees, tanks shooting at them and low-flying planes strafing them from the air.

As conditions grew worse, the Nazi authorities decided to relocate our school to a remote Bavarian mountain village called Schleching, nestled between the cities of Munich and Salzburg, to continue to keep us safe. We were to leave our host families behind and move to Schleching with our teachers.

We were losing our loved ones all over again. These people, on whom the accident of war had imposed us, had for the last year and a half been there when we were homesick, hungry or afraid, helped us with our homework, fed and clothed us. They had become our surrogate parents.

On the day of our departure, as my host mother Frau Vollmar helped me pack my few belongings, she placed a packet of home-baked biscuits in my bag. On top of the packet was a picture of the Vollmars and me, taken in the early days of my stay.

'Here, a little something to remember us by. Make sure to write to us often, you hear,' she admonished, waving her finger at me.

'Yes, Frau Vollmar, I will.'

I looked down, not wanting to betray the lump forming in my throat.

'All right then. You'll be just fine, you'll see.'

She turned and walked briskly out of the room. I finished packing alone. As I went out, getting ready to leave to meet my classmates and the teachers in front of the school, where we would be picked up by a bus, I bumped into the Vollmar children, who had been waiting in front of the door. The girls squeezed me with big hugs, and the boys punched me playfully in the shoulder and the stomach in a heartfelt goodbye. As I walked to school along the same path I had taken so many times before, a familiar feeling set in. I remembered sitting on my luggage at the dusty train station when I arrived in Konstanz so long ago, anxious and afraid, not knowing what was going to happen to me.

Later that evening, St Nicholas' Day, 6 December, under cover of night, the old bus we had all been piled into laboriously huffed its way up the winding mountain road to the Achental, where Schleching was. The slivers of light from the bus's dimmed headlights barely gave any view of the snow-covered road in front of us, just enough to make out the plunging darkness beyond the edge of the road. We finally arrived at the Hotel Zur Post, which was going to be our new home, but as we stumbled out of the bus, bone-tired, we heard: 'Boys, off you go to the shed over there to fill you a straw sack. It's going to be your mattress. Come on, we don't have all night.'

As unsurmountable as the task seemed, we nonetheless dutifully lined up to pick up sacks and stuffed as much straw into them as our tired arms could manage. Obedience was automatic, we did not question. Eventually, we dragged ourselves to our assigned rooms and collapsed into a dreamless sleep.

The food situation at Schleching was dire. The supply chain had been disrupted to such an extent that no food was reaching us anymore and we had to rely on whatever local sources were left, which wasn't much. There was virtually no arable land in mountain villages at these high elevations, only livestock, and the animals had been dwindling in number, consumed by the locals to survive. We were fed a watery bowl of cereal in the morning, followed by a thin gruel for lunch and the same for dinner. Once a week we were supposed to get some type of meat supplement, although more often than not we didn't. The thin gruel was never enough to quell the stabbing pains and cramps in our stomachs. The stuff ran right through us, leaving us weaker than before we had eaten it.

One fellow in our group, Willi Pampes, hailed from Herbeden, next to my hometown of Witten. His parents had sent him a food parcel, and by some miracle it actually arrived at Schleching. Since his parents were pig farmers, there was ham in the parcel. He kept cutting slices off it in front of us with his pocket-knife, making our mouths water, and would never give us any. But I had worked out where he hid it. One afternoon, when nobody was around, I sneaked into the dormitory, hurriedly pulled out the box he kept under his bunk bed behind his smelly shoes, took the ham out, cut off a big piece and devoured it right then and there because I was so hungry. The next day, Willi Pampes was upset about his reduced supply and kept asking everybody who the ham thief was.

'I will let you have some of my ham if you tell me who it is,' he cajoled, but the other kids just shrugged their shoulders.

They weren't very fond of him, since he had been flaunting his food in front of all of us and had never offered to share. Besides, I wasn't stupid and I hadn't told anybody what I had been up to. He never found out who did it.

Hunger was our constant companion and the defining condition that drove most of our actions. We needed more food and we were determined to find it. There was a butcher in the village who kept a big store of food in the cellar of his shop, sausages and hams hanging from the ceiling and all kinds of other food piled up on shelves – bread, tubes filled with cheese, and rich, creamy butter. Every time we found an opportunity we would sneak in at night and steal anything we could. We had found a back door leading to the cellar that didn't lock properly, although you could not tell, because the locking mechanism appeared to work unless you wiggled it a certain way. We would dump the hay out of the potato sacks that we used as pillows and take them with us to stuff our loot into. On the way back, we would sneak our booty up the stairs of the hotel in stockinged feet. We then wolfed the stuff down so it wouldn't be seen, suffering stomach cramps in the process; but the feeling of being full was well worth the pain.

On one of the nights that we went to steal food from the butcher we thought we were very clever and would play a prank. We filled a bucket of water, placed it on top of the door and connected it to the door with a cord which we looped over a hook, so that as soon as somebody came in, the bucket would topple over and drench him. It so happened that night that the butcher had realized someone was in his cellar and he rushed in yelling at us, but as soon as he crossed the threshold, all the water landed on his head.

'You little devils, just wait till I get my hands on you …' he spluttered, temporarily blinded by the water in his eyes. He was hopping mad, but while he was recovering from the shock and getting his bearings, we all ran away, laughing so hard our bellies hurt.

Unfortunately, that night we had to abandon our loot in our haste to escape, and we thought we would have to lie low for a little while until the butcher dropped his guard. As our supplies dwindled, hunger and cold were relentlessly tugging at our minds and bodies, threatening to bring us down. The little ones, only ten years old, had it worst. Some of them would wake crying from nightmares that had them reliving the separation from their parents. They were terrified they would never see them again. They looked up to us older boys, so we took on the role of big brothers, suppressing our own feelings of homesickness to appear strong in their eyes. We felt sorry for them but couldn't do much other than try to cheer them up once in a while.

One such occasion presented itself shortly after the aborted food run. One fellow in our class, Atti Schmiermann, was a particularly efficient food thief, so he still had a lot of provisions. But Atti had a particular condition; he suffered from night-blindness and had trouble orientating himself in the dark. One night, he suddenly had to urgently go and pee, but he couldn't find the door and started running around like a madman. Everybody began taunting him: 'Atti, hand over your sausages, or we don't turn on the lights.' But Atti wasn't about to give up his food. Instead, he pulled out his willy and started peeing in between the beds. Some unfortunate guy close to him got splashed, and then all hell broke loose.

He yelled, 'You dirty pig, you peed on me!'

Then everybody got excited, and a gigantic pillow fight ensued, some pillows becoming a bit damp in the process. Nobody got to eat Atti's food, but the little ones had fun that night.

One day in late February 1945, the sun finally broke through the cloud cover for the first time in three months, and the temperature was almost mild. We decided to go hiking to escape the feeling of having been cooped up all winter and climbed a mountain called the Geigelstein. We took turns racing up the steep incline, enjoying our newfound freedom, with stumbles and falls along the way. The valley below us, sparsely dotted with quaint wooden cabins still partially covered in snow, looked peaceful, like nothing bad could ever reach it.

When we arrived at the top, breathless and beaming with satisfaction that we had made it, we lay down to sunbathe. The sunshine felt pleasantly warm, despite there still being patches of snow on the ground. I must have fallen into a deep sleep for a while because when I woke up I was alone and found that some kid had removed my shoes. The sun was lower, and it had to be afternoon already. I stared down at the mountain trail that I would have to brave in bare feet, and I knew I had better get started because it was going to take a long time and I risked running out of daylight.

Without shoes, the path was steep and treacherous. I kept slipping and had to grab on to rocks to catch myself, every time wincing at the pain of the sharp stones and brambles embedding themselves in my feet as I struggled for purchase, and scraping my soles in trying to secure a foothold so I wouldn't tumble down the mountain. When I finally got to the bottom I could hardly walk any more, my feet were so raw and bloody. As I limped into the village, a kid who had been on the hike informed on the culprit, probably expecting to witness a good show when I got my hands on him. The prankster's name was Karl Hasenkamm. His parents owned a bar in Witten, close to my parents' house.

'You just wait …' I hissed as I passed the kid in search of Karl.

The kid followed me.

I found Karl walking down the street with some classmates, my shoes dangling around his neck tied together by their shoelaces.

'Hey, idiot,' I called out.

'What?' he countered, stopping in the middle of the street with a swagger, trying to impress his friends.

I walked up to him, adrenalin pumping so hard I didn't feel the pain in my feet. He didn't see the punch coming. I hit him so hard I knocked him off his feet, and my shoes flew off his neck on to the ground. A circle formed around us, the other kids egging us on. He scrambled up and lunged at me head-first, gripping me like a wrestler, trying to make me fall. I prised him off me. He swiped at my head, missed and grabbed me again. I pushed him off, and when he charged back, I hit him again, so hard that he flew back, fell and, this time, didn't get back up.

'That's what, arsehole', I said, picked up my shoes, and walked away with a slight limp but with my head held high, leaving him on the ground moaning.

I was pretty sure he'd think twice about having fun at my expense again.

Chapter 15

The SS

In early March, the same Waffen-SS Panzer troops who had visited us in Konstanz and picked my two pals and me for the arms training arrived in Schleching. They occupied the village, along with regular military forces who took over our small classrooms. We knew this meant Schleching was now potentially in the line of fire. I realized with a start that this could mean that we might actually have to serve, that it hadn't all been just a drill.

By this time any connection to our parents had been completely severed. The distances were too great, the postal system didn't work any more because the Allies had been bombing the train tracks, and as a result our parents didn't know where we were. We were isolated from everything, and now the SS were here. They seemed to be everywhere we turned, asking questions, observing our every move, making us uncomfortable. They showed us newsreels of the Führer's speeches. He said we were a superior race, destined to rule. We were not to waste time with those who were our intellectual and biological inferiors. The German nation was at war with enemies who wanted to destroy it, but they would fail, because the German soldier could not be defeated.

'Boys, soon it will be your turn. The Führer counts on you. We will tell you a secret,' an SS officer said to us one afternoon after class.

We perked up, curious to hear more.

'The Führer, whom you have everything to thank for, has developed the *Wunderwaffe*, the miracle weapon, for the German people.'

He paused for effect. We gasped.

The SS officer raised his voice. 'The *Wunderwaffe* will be deployed in all its might and will lay waste to the enemy, and we will be there to witness the final blow.'

Speechless, we looked at each other in wonder, our imaginations on fire at the might of the German Reich.

Every time the SS officers entered a room, or whenever we came across one of them, we had to stand at attention and salute vigorously with our right hand shooting straight up in front of us, loudly and decisively shouting, 'Heil Hitler!' Anything short of enthusiasm would have been interpreted as lack of conviction, and we knew that we would be punished for it, because the SS was extremely strict in enforcing loyalty to our Führer. They had made it clear to us that lack of full support for and obedience to the Führer's benevolent rule was ungrateful and treasonable and would not be tolerated. In the letters we got from our parents, before they stopped arriving, we had heard of people who weren't convincing enough in their devotion to the Führer being taken away for questioning; some didn't come back. Then there was our neighbour, Herr Herrman, who owned a tailor's shop and had complained about the SS. Mama wrote that he had stopped getting any business and had to close his shop. He and his family had to rely on their help and that of other neighbours to eat, because for some reason he couldn't get food stamps anymore. I thought back, with an uneasy feeling in the pit of my stomach, to the time I was interrogated at the station.

The food situation had now become dire. We were reduced to being fed a thin, watery gruel in the morning and beetroot soup for lunch, day in and day out, until we wanted to puke at the sight of it. At night we got a thin slice of hard black bread. Now that the SS and the soldiers were there, our lives became a lot more complicated, because we were being closely monitored; if we got caught stealing we knew we would be severely punished. We had been told that misbehaviour would not be tolerated, but our hunger emboldened us and made us reckless.

There was a close call one evening with one of the younger kids who had stuffed a bunch of packaged cheese tubes he had stolen from the butcher's in his knickerbockers. It wasn't very late, and it turned out that some adults had not yet retired for the night. As he was running up the stairs, one of the buckles that fastened the knickerbockers to his legs came loose and the cheese tubes slipped out and went tumbling down the stairs, thump, thump, thump. All of us who were running up the stairs behind him with our own loot froze in place. Luckily, the innkeeper lady noticed what was going on and managed to distract an officer who thought he had heard something by sending him off in another direction, giving the kid and the rest of us time to scramble out of danger.

Next to the Hotel Zur Post was the post office. The SS had set up shop there and were storing provisions in the building. We hungrily watched them transporting boxes upon boxes full of food inside.

One night, a kid from our group sneaked into the SS depot and swiped some butter and ham. Nobody realized how different this act was from what we had done before. The risk of being caught was always there, and we had known there would be a punishment – perhaps we would be beaten, made to perform menial chores or not fed for a few days – but somehow we still did it because the stomach cramps were too painful to bear. But the SS played by different rules and they were keeping watch. They caught the kid red-handed. It turned out that stealing from the SS carried the death penalty by firing squad. This was something we had not known. Although rumours of their ruthless discipline abounded, the extent of the threat had not fully registered before. Once a different outcome might have been possible, but by early 1945 any vestige of clemency was gone and had long since given way to increasingly erratic and violent behaviour by Hitler's forces.

Our headmaster desperately tried to intercede on the boy's behalf and pleaded with the SS to spare him. They had the younger kids believe that they sent him away to serve his punishment elsewhere.

They sent the little ones somewhere early the next morning on a field trip, but they left us older ones, thirteen and up, behind. We were to be taught a lesson.

It happened quickly and matter-of-factly. It was a bleak, cold spring morning, the smell of snow still in the air. As soon as the young ones were gone, they lined the rest of us up in the dining room and told us: 'Boys, today you will witness the Führer's justice. The Hitler Youth upholds the highest standards of Aryan conduct. Criminal behaviour shall not be tolerated and will be rooted out without hesitation. We will not allow a bad seed to infect others. He who steals from the Führer deserves to die.'

My mind fought against the meaning of the words I heard, my blood running cold. I didn't dare look at anybody. We were instructed to keep what we saw to ourselves and not tell the younger children, or we would pay for our disobedience. It would not have occurred to us to disobey. Without delay, they marched us outside in the bitter cold and had us stand obliquely facing the wall of the back of the hotel building.

Directly facing the wall was the firing squad, maybe four men. They dragged the kid out from somewhere, blindfolded and with his hands tied behind his back, stood him against the wall and left him there. He was whimpering. A voice shouted an order. A deafening fusillade of shots tore through the air. The sharp cracking noise, so much louder than I had imagined, made me jump out of my skin. Blood spattered on the white wall behind the kid, and he just fell like a rag doll. A wave of nausea engulfed me, but sheer terror prevented me from moving a single muscle. I was rooted to the ground. Somehow we were marched back inside the building. I don't remember getting inside or anything else about that day, but the image of what I saw had indelibly burned itself into my consciousness with agonizing clarity. We never spoke again of what had happened.

A few days later, the time finally came for the three of us who had had the weapons training a few months earlier to pay our dues. The SS walked into the classroom, called our names and motioned for us to follow them out to the hallway. We looked at each other in wide-eyed alarm. But we had no choice, so we filed out of the classroom. I was trying hard not to tremble. Once outside, one of the officers asked us where we wanted to go.

Nervous and confused by the question, we blurted out in unison, 'Nowhere, sir. We don't want to go anywhere. We want to stay in Schleching, in school, sir.'

The commander in charge straightened his stance. His left hand gripped his polished silver belt buckle so tightly that I noticed his knuckles turning white. He took a deep breath, as if to compose himself, the corner of his lip twitching, and stepped closer. My skin was crawling. Finally, he addressed us with an air of mildly annoyed benevolence, as if speaking to dim-witted children.

'No, the choice is a different one. You can choose between two things. You either come with us to the SS, where you get good meals, warm beds and time off to see your parents,' he promised, 'or you can go into the Wehrmacht, the German military forces.'

By that he meant the normal military that was not subordinated to the SS. The choice was easy. We had seen enough. Wanting nothing to do with these creeps from the SS, we were deeply relieved to be offered a chance to get as far away from them as we possibly could. We glanced at each other only for a split second and unanimously replied, 'We would like to sign up for the regular military, sir.'

The commander grimaced.

'Very well then, if that is your decision.'

He stomped off stiffly, leaving us standing there. It was obvious the SS were not happy with this outcome, but they had given us the choice, and we had made it.

We were shipped out of Schleching to meet up with the Wehrmacht on 18 March 1945. The very next day, 19 March, the Allies bombed and completely destroyed my home town of Witten. The illegal ham radios we had in Schleching informed my schoolmates of what happened, but since my two comrades and I had just left, I did not find out about it until the day I finally returned home, a long time afterwards.

Chapter 16

Heldentot

As the SS military transport we were travelling in approached the meeting point with the Wehrmacht, the deep rumbling and muffled booming sounds of artillery fire reverberated through the metal skin of the vehicle and shook my body. I said a silent prayer.

General Walter von Unruh was known in Germany as 'General *Heldenklau*', (General Hero-Thief), because he was always on the lookout for good candidates to join his *Panzerbekämpfungstruppen*, anti-tank troops. The SS was driving me and my schoolmates Helmut and Knapsack from Schleching to the closest meeting point with the Wehrmacht, which happened to be where the general was at the time. He was visiting units close to the Eastern Front, probably to boost morale among the troops.

The general had apparently been informed of our arrival and he took an interest in us. We were told by the SS during the drive that we would be meeting him, and we had been rooted in place ever since, petrified at the thought of finding ourselves in the presence of this famous soldier. He drove up to us in his jeep, or the equivalent German vehicle, and got out to inspect us. The chest of his impeccable grey uniform was covered with gleaming medals, the black visor of his officer's hat was polished to a fault. We stood stiffly at attention, not daring to blink or breathe as he approached. He had distinguished himself so much in the First World War that Hitler appointed him to be the recruiter-in-chief for all the armed forces of the Reich. Although quite an old man, he was not bent but had the stiff, proud bearing of a Prussian soldier. We were in awe of him, but he was friendly as he talked to us, making us feel a little more at ease.

'*Jungens*, come with me.'

He motioned to us to join him in his vehicle and said he was taking us to his troops in the south of Bavaria, a fully motorized Panzer unit. The three of us jumped into the back seat.

'You will experience the full might of the German armed forces. You get to be part of it,' he said, turning to us with a smile.

The whole thing felt like a movie to us – we were driving in a fast car with a famous general who was making conversation with us. I could hardly believe my luck. People would have given anything to be in the presence of such a legend. Knapsack elbowed me in the ribs, grinning from ear to ear, fidgeting in his seat like a five-year-old. I elbowed him back, looking at him sternly in an attempt to make him stop so we could pretend to look composed. His open-mouthed grin only got wider, and I knew it was a lost cause.

When we arrived we were immediately shown to temporary barracks and issued with uniforms. We were mobilizing the same day, so there was no time to waste. The order had been given that we were to go to the city of Wiener Neustadt, because a great tank attack by the Bolsheviks was expected, and since we were in the *Panzerjägereinheit*, the tank-hunter unit, we were being sent down to meet them. The makeshift buildings were swiftly dismantled and loaded on trucks, and we were soon on our way. An entire base had been undone in front of our eyes in mere minutes, and it looked like nothing had ever been there before. We gawked in open-mouthed admiration at the efficiency of a German military operation in action.

We rode in a *Steuermannschaftswagen*, a military transport vehicle; the driver and the lieutenant sat in front, and in the back there was space for three guys to sit on benches along the right side and another three guys on the left. A removable tarpaulin covered the back. My two pals and I sat on one side. The other three guys in the truck were new boys, too.

'Hey,' they nodded at us.

'Hey,' we nodded back.

'Been in battle already?' we asked.

'No, we just got here,' one of them answered.

They were *Flakhelfer*, anti-aircraft gunners, part of a military force almost entirely made up of teenage boys. Every schoolboy who reached the age of sixteen was enrolled as a *Flakhelfer*. They were not engaged in active battle but manned the anti-aircraft guns that shot down enemy planes. Once the *Flakhelfer* turned eighteen, they were automatically drafted into active military service. All the new young recruits at this stage in the war were either *Flakhelfer* or, like us, pulled from the *Kinderlandverschickung*, the children's relocation programme. My two pals from Konstanz and I, at fourteen years old, were the youngest.

'And you chaps?' asked the boy who had told us who they were.

'We're from the KLV,' I answered.

'No, really? I didn't think they took you this young.'

I just shrugged and sat up straighter, not wanting him to think we were little kids.

Behind us in the convoy came the *Panzerabwehrkanonenwagen*, the trucks hauling the 88mm anti-tank cannon. There were several of these, followed by more personnel carriers. Everybody had been issued their weapons, a pistol and a *Sturmgewehr*, the automatic machine gun. The ammunition hung along both sides of the vehicle. When you were out of ammo, you took the empty magazine out and shoved another one in.

The *Panzerfäuste* were stored in a bucket in the truck bed. The *Panzerfaust* was a fearsome weapon that had the ability, if accurately fired, to penetrate the front of a tank and explode inside it. We had been trained to use it at camp and had been advised of its deadliness. Remembering the training, I watched the weapons swaying in the bucket with a touch of apprehension, even though I knew they couldn't go off that way.

On our way to Wiener Neustadt from southern Bavaria we passed through the city of Bischofshofen. As we were driving through town we came upon an old market square in the middle of the city which had a wine cellar. We stopped the trucks and got off, and everybody cheerily agreed, 'Aha, we've got to go in there and drink a little wine.'

By then we had adopted a bit of a *'Landsknecht'* (mercenary) mentality. It had been drilled into us that when a German man is in uniform and carries a weapon, he is stronger than anything and anybody else. Now we boys were wearing uniforms and carrying weapons. With the new identity we acquired by donning this gear, which resembled what we had been shown so often in the glorious weekly news accounts of our heroes, we somehow believed ourselves all-powerful.

We went up to the door, only to discover that the wine cellar was locked. As we were attempting to force the door open, an Austrian man came running and shouted, 'Hey, that is our wine cellar! You can't go in there.'

I turned around, pointed my *Sturmgewehr* at the guy and told him, 'You, come here and open the wine cellar. Now!' waving him on with my gun.

The other guys gave me approving looks.

Coincidentally, the man happened to have the key. Unhappily, he opened the door, and we walked down the steep medieval steps into the ancient bowels of the cellar and went to work on the wine. It happened to be an extremely warm day. There was a dry Föhn wind blowing from the valley which made for awfully hot weather, and here we were in this nice cool wine cellar getting completely hammered. We belted patriotic songs off-key and toasted the great future victories we had been promised. Since we wanted to take some of the wine with us, we took our canteens – all soldiers carried water bottles – poured out the water and replaced it with wine. Once everybody had filled up, we made our way up the stairs, but as we emerged from the cold cellar into the strangely hot air, I, along with a couple of others, fell flat on my face at the top of the steps. I was so drunk I didn't even feel my face slam into the pavement. Before that day I had never tasted a drop of alcohol, and it had quite an effect on me. Once I managed to pick myself up and recover my composure as best I could, I spotted the Austrian who had been waiting outside. With a marked slur in my speech, rather unsteady on my feet, I gave him an order.

'You … you should damn well lock your wine cellar back up because we have to continue on. After all, the German Reich needs to be protected from the Bolsheviks!'

The Austrian, shaking his head, locked up his wine cellar while I strutted away in as dignified a manner as I could muster, concentrating hard on walking in a straight line. All of us piled into our *Mannschaftswagen* and continued to drive in the direction of Wiener Neustadt.

After travelling for about ten or twenty kilometres we stopped at an inn to get some lunch. As soldiers we got to eat whatever was being served without being charged. We ate schnitzel and potatoes to our heart's content, a wonderful meal that put us in a relaxed and mellow mood. Our bellies were full, and we were still a little drunk, so when we got back into the truck I slumped down in my corner, leaned my head back against the wall, my buzz-cut hair grazing the steel helmet hanging from a peg just above me, and promptly went to sleep.

Previously, on one of the stops we had made along the way on the road from South Bavaria, my pal Knapsack had found a Russian machine gun lying in a field and had taken it with him. Knapsack was not his actual name, of course; it was a nickname he had acquired in school, but its use became so universal that at some point nobody could remember what he was actually called. He was a big guy, pretty strongly built, but he was not exactly the brightest light in the shed. Beside the Russian machine gun, Knapsack had also found a Russian cap of leather, with thick fur lining the inside to protect its wearer from the bitter winter cold.

When he found the cap he put it on and announced with a wide grin, 'Look what I got.'

'Oh, look, here comes General Vlasov,' joked one of the guys.

From that point on we called Knapsack 'Vlasov'. This was a famous Russian general who had joined the Byelorussian forces to fight against the Bolsheviks. He used to wear a cap very much like the one our friend Knapsack was sporting, which made him resemble the pictures we had seen of the Russian general. He didn't seem to mind the comparison and kept wearing the cap even though the weather was stiflingly hot. It didn't make him look any smarter.

While I was sleeping off my meal and the alcohol, Vlasov was messing around with his Russian machine gun. He was sitting right across from me.

Suddenly, *rat-tat-tat-tat-tat*! the machine gun went off in a spasm. I started awake and felt the wind on my scalp as one bullet whistled just above my short-cropped hair, then heard all the other bullets loudly striking my steel helmet, riddling it with holes. In that split second I just stared at Knapsack, stupefied. In the blink of an eye, the other guys jumped on him, took the machine gun away from him and secured the weapon. The lieutenant came running in from the driver's cabin.

'What the hell just happened in here?' he demanded, taking in the situation at a glance.

'Sir ... he ... he had the machine gun, sir, and he was messing around with it and it went off, and Willi almost got hit, sir. And then we jumped him and took the gun from him.'

The lieutenant bore down on Knapsack. 'You dumb, good-for-nothing, ignorant moron. You could have killed everybody! Haven't you learned a damned thing in your training? You idiot, don't you know how to disarm a weapon?'

Knapsack's punishment was cleaning the truck, carrying everybody's heavy equipment, cleaning all the weapons, and other menial tasks. But mentally, he was not all right. He was so pale with fright that he looked like a ghost, and so spooked that he lost his ability to speak and didn't utter a single word for three days. I could almost have felt sorry for him if I hadn't been so angry. If he had not missed my head by less than a centimetre, I would have died that day the so-called *Heldentot*, the hero's death. That's how it was with the Nazis; if somebody died accidentally, he was celebrated in the homeland like a national hero. A consolation for the relatives, I suppose. As the full realization of what had almost happened sank in, I couldn't help but think with dread in my heart how horrible it would have been if a dumb idiot like Knapsack had taken me out; that would have been it for me. It also gave me my first inkling of the randomness of war, of the burden of knowledge every soldier carries that in the end everything is down to chance; that at any moment a stray bullet, a false step on a mine, fire from the air or some other violent event can end your life with no rhyme or reason.

As we advanced deeper into Austrian territory through the Steiermark region we kept a lookout for the enemy, but we saw no Americans – we called them 'Amis' – and no Russians anywhere. We were moving through no-man's-land in Austria, and everything looked quiet. This lifted our spirits and we let down our guard a bit, thinking things weren't so bad after all.

Unfortunately, we rejoiced a little too soon.

The Battle of Vienna (29 March – 13 April 1945)

On 30 March 1945, Soviet troops crossed into Austria near Koszeg in Hungary, only 50 miles from Vienna. Between 1 and 2 April they captured Wiener Neustadt and other neighbouring towns, threatening to advance further. On 3 April the Soviet 2nd Ukrainian Front penetrated the German defensive lines between Wiener Neustadt and Neusiedler Lake and started advancing toward Vienna.

Liezen city chronicler Rudolf Polzer described how in the last days of the war, and especially in the period from 8 to 11 May, 1945, soldiers of the dissolving German Wehrmacht as well as extremely large numbers of civilians from Hungary and Yugoslavia streamed into the town from the south and southeast, as it had become known that the Enns River, which ran through Liezen, was to serve as a demarcation line between the Soviets and the Americans. The German troops as well as the civilians were desperate to escape from the Red Army.

While the US troops arrived in Liezen on 8 May, the Red Army did not reach the established border until 11 May.

Part III

Total War

Chapter 17

The Last Bullet

As we approached Wiener Neustadt to engage the Russians on 31 March 1945, I saw the majestic Neusiedler Lake straddling the Austro-Hungarian border in the distance. Something in that beautiful but unfamiliar view reminded me how far I was from home. For a moment I was back at Opa Johannes' farm, running through the tall wheat fields that swayed and rolled in the wind like soft golden waves. Suddenly it all became real. A chill ran up my spine, making the hair stand on end at the back of my neck. I squirmed uncomfortably in my seat, my body willing me to jump off the moving truck. But I couldn't do that. I couldn't turn back and leave. I was trapped. I was coming inexorably closer to the war, whether I wanted to or not. At that moment it became clear to me that didn't want to be there. I just wanted to go home.

Our convoy slowly approached the front line. The sky was leaden, moisture was in the air from recent rain. We reached an open field that was a muddy mess from being trampled by the troops and equipment of the Panzer unit. Everything was abuzz with activity. Trucks, tanks and guns were moving around everywhere, seemingly without a clear direction, although I felt there had to be a purpose to all the movement that I just could not discern. I swallowed hard. This was it, this was the front, and I was going to fight my first battle.

Suddenly I heard the first real cannon fire I had ever heard in my life up close. It was a blast so strong that my feet lifted off the ground, my heart jumped out of my chest and my hero's blood no longer ran red. My hero's blood ran brown, because I was so scared that I shat my pants. Not having another uniform to change into, I had to drop my trousers and make do with some grass to wipe off what I could and get on with it.

Everybody who had arrived in the convoy was dispatched to the front line with shovels. Our leaders knew more or less where the Russians were going to come from, and we, the tank-hunters, were told to dig deep holes in the ground. We were to make the holes as deep as we were tall, so that we could stand in them. The terrain was flat, but the ground was damp, making it difficult to dig because the soil was heavy with moisture. We struggled to get the job done.

As we dug, we had taken off our *Sturmgewehre* and our *Panzerfäuste*, but we kept the weapons next to us.

'*Los, los, Kameraden!*' shouted the lieutenant with urgency.

Time was of the essence. We dug faster.

Eventually we were done, and we nodded at each other before climbing down into our holes. We could just barely see over the tops of them. Behind us, we were told, was the Italian Bersaglieri light infantry division. They were supposed to spring into action once the Russian tanks were hit, which is when the Russian infantry armed with bayonets would emerge from behind the tanks to fight the German *Panzerjäger* on the ground. This Italian unit was supposed to march forward and stop the Russian grenadiers advancing. That was the plan. However, the Italians' loyalties had been divided since 1943, when their Prime Minister Marshal Pietro Badoglio had negotiated a cease-fire with the Americans, the British and the French, and an Italian expeditionary corps had joined the Allied forces to fight the Germans. We were a bit concerned as to what extent the knowledge of this situation might influence the actions of our good Italian Bersaglieri friends standing behind us on that fateful day.

We stood in the holes we had dug, about ten metres apart. In each of them there was a man, or a fourteen-year-old boy like me.

We each had four *Panzerfäuste* with us. Since this was a single-shot weapon we prayed we'd have enough time to run back to the supply truck to get more in case we ran out and there were more tanks coming.

We stood quietly in our holes. Each of us was alone with his thoughts, not knowing if they would be his last. Sound was amplified in the oppressive silence, and with my senses heightened, I could hear the rustle of leaves on nearby trees and my neighbour shuffling his feet. Time was running out.

I felt the ground vibrate. A growl so deep it hurt my ears filled the air, increasing in intensity. Then a dark wall of tanks appeared over the horizon, advancing fast. There were too many to count. I swallowed.

We had been given clear instructions by our officers: 'Let the tank advance to a distance of exactly twenty metres from you, no more, no less.'

You had one shot at this.

I was an excellent marksman. I raised the *Panzerfaust* on to my right shoulder, tucked it under my armpit, waited until the first tank reached the white boulder I had mentally pegged as the twenty-metre mark, aimed quickly and shot off my first shell. I held my breath for a split second. The shell penetrated the hull of the tank and the tank exploded, just as we had been told it would. It burst into flames right in front of me, so close that I felt a wave of heat hit my face. My comrades were firing, too, but it seemed to make no difference. More and more tanks came at us. The blasts were deafening, the air heavy with the smell of burnt metal and flesh. To my right, a tank drove straight toward the hole of a fellow soldier. The tank stopped over the hole and swivelled around in a circle on its own axis twice, grinding itself into the ground; I watched in helpless horror while the poor fellow's shrill screams pierced my skull. After a moment he stopped screaming. The tank had crushed him. I knew that guy; he was one of the *Flakhelfer* from the military vehicle. Another *Panzerjäger* delivered a fatal shot to the tank.

Breathless, I quickly refocused my attention on what was in front of me to avoid suffering the same fate. There was no time to mourn my friend. Just in the nick of time I shot a second tank that was fast approaching, but they kept coming, and we kept shooting. We were vastly outnumbered. The wall of tanks was upon us despite our desperate efforts to stave them off, then from behind their shadow the grenadiers emerged and charged in force with their bayonets. The Italian Bersaglieri who were supposed to have our backs were nowhere in sight. I knew I had to get out of the hole, but not before taking out as many Russians as possible with my *Sturmgewehr*. I started shooting. The other fellows did the same thing as the grenadiers continued to advance, some falling dead or wounded along the way, the rest of them marching on to fulfil their mission, impervious to the fate of their fallen comrades.

A burst of hot air scorched my left cheek. I shot a glance in the direction of the searing heat, scanning for the nearest foxhole. My mind did not immediately comprehend what I saw. Blood was spouting from a headless body in pulsating spurts where my comrade had stood just a minute ago. His head was missing. A frozen grip closed my throat as I stared at what had been my friend, draining me of all strength and will, as if the blood leaving the dismembered body were my own.

A shell blasted off nearby. The sound shook me out of my stupor, and I tore my gaze away, electrified by the instinct to survive. I could no longer keep the Russians at bay as I had no more ammunition for the *Sturmgewehr*. I only had my pistol left. The SS had taught us: 'Comrades, take care when you are at the front, and save the last bullet for yourselves. To fall into Russian hands and become a prisoner of war is a fate worse than death, because they torture people.'

The Russians had closed in on us. I scrambled out of the hole and shot at the grenadiers with my pistol, but I ran out of ammunition and was left with one last bullet. I looked down at it in a moment of indecision. *Now what?*

I looked up. There was a Russian in front of me.

He pointed his bayonet and thrust it toward my belly. I quickly grabbed the *Sturmgewehr* which was slung over my shoulder and shoved it at his bayonet, blocking it, so that his thrust was diverted from my belly to my left leg, the blade of the weapon slicing my leg open from knee to ankle. Blood gushed out of my wound. I looked up, and for a brief instant I hesitated. The Russian grenadier was a young kid just like me; he had straw-blond hair like so many Russians, clear blue eyes and the high cheekbones typical of Slavs. We made eye contact. I saw no malice in him, just a guy doing what he was told. As he recovered his wits and struggled to dislodge his weapon from my leg, I fired my last bullet into his head.

Dazed, sitting next to the dead Russian boy and bleeding profusely, I looked behind me, waiting for the Italian infantry to finally show up and close with the Russian grenadiers. I could hear distantly shouted orders over the infernal din of guns and screams around me: 'Retreat! Fall back!'

I kept looking behind me and didn't see a soul. Nobody was coming to the rescue. It was then I realized I had better start running. Blood was pumping out of my knee in spurts, and I was becoming weaker and weaker with every step I took. Two of my pals saw me and ran over to help.

'Willi, we've got you, hold on!'

One guy grabbed my arm and slung it over his shoulders, half dragging me, half helping me run. While we ran, the other guy tore his shirt into shreds and applied a tourniquet to my leg, above and below the wound, and tried to stop the bleeding by stuffing fabric into the cut, everything at a mad scrambling pace to get away from the front line. I was becoming lightheaded, but they kept pushing me on.

'Come on, Willi, you can do this. We're almost there.'

I groaned. I was dead tired, but somehow my legs kept moving. We ran and ran and ran, until eventually we made it through a forest, behind which was another German unit, infantry with light cannon who were being sent forward to continue the battle.

'Hey, this guy is hurt. He needs help!' shouted my comrades as we approached.

A couple of medics showed up and carried me to a cot. I felt so grateful I could finally rest. For lack of anything else to hand, they poured horse urine, rich in ammonia and known to have antiseptic properties, on my wound to disinfect it. There, in the makeshift field hospital, my leg was precariously stitched up, leaving a very large, ragged scar on my left leg. I fell into a dreamless sleep of exhaustion.

The next day, together with the other guys whose injuries had been patched up, I was considered fit enough to be 'allowed' to re-engage in combat. It didn't feel like such a privilege to me, but it was my duty. My country needed me. It was 1 April, and the Soviet 2nd Ukrainian Front had advanced to capture Wiener Neustadt.

As we were trying to hold our position against the Russians near Wiener Neustadt we engaged in further battles, and I blew up a few more Russian T-34 tanks with my *Panzerfäuste*. By 3 April, however, the Soviet 2nd Ukrainian Front had penetrated the German defensive lines between Wiener Neustadt and Neusiedler Lake, advancing toward Vienna. Even though at this point we were starting to retreat, my comrades and I were recommended for the Iron Cross 2nd class for our bravery on the field of battle. As I had destroyed ten tanks I received ten stripes on my uniform. There was a tank drawn on each of the stripes. I had eight tanks on my left sleeve and two on my right. I thought back wistfully to my target practice instructor at *Jungvolk* who had said, 'This is the way we show the enemy we are superior, and how we bring them to their knees. This is the quality of the elite troops we produce, that the world fears and that make our Führer proud – Heil Hitler!'

Maybe we had failed to defeat them, but I had given it my all.

We were presented with the Iron Cross 2nd class somewhere in an open field, close to where the fighting was, clearly to boost our morale. An elevated podium was set up, the swastika flags flanking it on each side, and the troops were lined up in close ranks facing the stage. The ceremony was filmed, probably with the aim of including it in the *Wochenschauen*, the weekly newsreels shown in cinemas around the country which spoke only of German victories. I remembered the many *Wochenschauen* I had watched back at camp, star-struck, marvelling at the superior German forces, imagining myself as part of them, engaged in heroic actions. And here I was now, battered and tired, a bit the worse for the wear, but soberly resolved to do my duty to my country.

The mighty *Reichsfeldmarschall* Hermann Göring himself had travelled there in person and called us forward to present us with the Iron Cross. Göring was the spokesman for Adolf Hitler, but rumour had it that he had fallen out of favour. It was said that he had moved to southern Germany with people loyal to him and was independently promoting soldiers, acting as if he were the Führer's successor. Perhaps he went a bit crazy, and perhaps we were taking part in one of the ceremonies that he was staging independently, without Hitler's approval. If that were true, it meant we would never make the *Wochenschau*. I thought that was a shame. We would never find out.

The Iron Cross we received at his hands was a group distinction, which means we did not individually receive a physical medal, but we were honoured nonetheless. It was the ultimate symbol of valour and service to the homeland. My chest filled with pride. Göring's strategy worked. He reminded us to defend our Fatherland from the enemy to the death and, caught in the transcendence of the moment, we wholeheartedly vowed to do so.

Chapter 18

The Retreat

Events were rapidly overtaking us. Shortly after the ceremony, our officers received the order to retreat as quickly as possible from the front lines. Vienna had been taken. We were to move quickly due west to the town of Liezen in the Steiermark region of Austria. This was ominous news. The Russians were at Germany's doorstep, yet we were pulling back. Could it be that we were losing the war? It seemed utterly unthinkable, and yet I had experienced the overwhelming assault of the Red Army on my own body. A jolt of fear sharpened my senses. If it was true that we were losing, giving ourselves up to the Allied Forces was our only option if we wanted a chance of staying alive. Our officers had told us that we could not allow ourselves to be taken prisoner by the Russians because they would torture and kill us. But were they going to lead us to the Americans, or to our heroes' deaths?

While the Wehrmacht had managed to slow down the advance of the Bolsheviks, who were closing in from the south-east, they had been retreating from the Americans, who were closing in from the north. We overheard muted discussions among the officers.

'"It's over. We must find them. No other choice." That is what I heard the lieutenant say to the *Oberst* [colonel],' my pal Helmut reported to a small group of us.

So, it was true. We had listened intently, almost hopefully, to his account. 'Are you sure that's what he said?' somebody asked. Did this mean our leaders were going to try to get us to the Americans, even if that meant surrendering? Nobody dared say out loud what was on his mind; it was a heretical thought, punishable by death. Yet the conclusion seemed inevitable.

We didn't leave without a fight. What was left of our unit destroyed a few more Russian tanks in a couple of skirmishes, and then we pushed off and moved due north-west, as planned. We drove off in a rush with the aim of reaching the town of Liezen. As it turned out, we were not alone. We were joining a swelling tide of soldiers from our disintegrating forces, as well as civilians from Yugoslavia and Hungary, all trying to get north of the River Enns that runs through Liezen which, our command had been informed, was to become the demarcation line between the Bolsheviks and the Americans. We heard that the Reich was to be divided between the Allies and the Bolsheviks, and anybody caught south of the river would be stuck under Russian rule. I had seen enough these last few weeks to know what that fate looked like, and I fervently hoped we would make it across the line in time. The tide had turned. Our dreams of victory had been replaced by nightmares of defeat. A sense of urgency set in, and sheer survival instinct took over.

The Enns ran along the southern edge of the city. Our single-minded goal was to get there before the Russians did. We knew that the Red Army would take no prisoners, and the Russians were ahead of us, to judge from the destruction we found on our path. Our strategy was to sidestep them and then beat them to the target. At this point we were an exhausted and hungry bunch, hanging on by sheer willpower. Nobody in their right mind believed any more that the war could be won, although still nobody dared to say it out loud lest he be put to death for treason to the Führer and the Fatherland. We all just hoped to somehow make it out alive.

As we made our way north-west towards American-controlled territory we passed many towns that had been razed by the Russians as they had made their way north to liberate Vienna. From the few civilian survivors we were hearing accounts of extreme brutality by Russian soldiers and of violence against German women. Later reports estimated that two million German women were raped, 100,000 in Berlin alone.

As we approached one town which had been taken back by our troops we could see the damaged buildings ahead. The town appeared deserted. The afternoon sun was hazy, everything eerily quiet. An acrid smell hung in the air, a mixture of burnt rubber, metal, gunpowder and decay.

We drove on and approached a Catholic convent on a hill on the outskirts of the town. The air was thick with a sickly-sweet odour, and flies were buzzing about. The building had been heavily damaged by fire, and smoke was still emanating from the ruins. A stray dog ran loose on the road. The soot-covered old walls of the compound looked ominous to me. When we turned the corner to the front of the building we saw that the massive wooden front gates were wide open. There was a German military truck parked in front of them, but nobody seemed to be inside the vehicle. Our lieutenant ordered us to stop.

As we got off the truck, the stench intensified. My stomach turned over. We approached the gates and saw a couple of German soldiers standing motionless in the middle of the open courtyard, looking down at something on the ground. We walked through the gates. At first, I could not make out what I was looking at; it looked like burst-open potato sacks. When I focused more closely, my brain finally made sense of the images before me.

The lifeless bodies of the nuns were strewn about like broken dolls twisted at impossible angles, gutted like pigs from neck to groin, their entrails exposed in macabre glistening piles, their black and white habits stiff with dried blood. Their dead eyes stared unseeingly at the sky, and their mouths were open in agonized grimaces, as if locked in one last desperate prayer to a God who had not heeded their call. What else had been done to them was plainly obvious. They had been brutally raped, defiled in every possible way. It defied all description. My stomach lurched violently, and I ran to a corner. Bent over, I threw up until only bile came out, but still I kept heaving. I needed to get everything out, but I could not clean my mind or my body from this horror no matter how hard I tried. As I crouched there I sensed a presence behind me. It was my lieutenant. He put his hand on my shoulder, and said in a quiet voice:

'*Komm*, Langbein, we can't help anybody here anymore. It's time to go.'

As we continued on our way we learned what the SS, these pieces of shit, were doing to poor German soldiers who didn't know where to go. When the SS saw a German soldier wandering around they'd ask, 'Where is your unit?' and he'd inevitably say something like, 'I don't know. We have all been dispersed.'

Without hesitation, they would then seize the poor lad, who didn't understand what was going on, and before he knew what was about to happen, they would tie a rope around his neck and hang him from the nearest tree. Loyalty to the Führer was to the end of life, and the only choices for a German soldier were victory or death. Surrender was not an option. A wandering soldier was therefore a deserter and a coward and had to be executed. We saw the grim evidence as we passed through a small town; a young German soldier was hanging from a tree beside the road. The civilians had warned us about this as we entered the town, but when I saw his lifeless body dangling from a branch like a discarded doll, I realized with horror that this is what had become of the proud German Reich.

Soon enough we ourselves were to witness the SS at work. We were driving through the next town, the name of which I never knew because they had all started blurring together in my mind, on our way towards Liezen. We had stopped our convoy to try to obtain provisions from the civilians and saw droves of people so frightened of the advancing Red Army that they were leaving on foot or on bicycles with just the clothes on their back, heading west in search of safety. Many looked at us in dismay and sadness, conscious that we could no longer effectively defend them. Half of our small squad, around six men, were on foot with our lieutenant when we saw two Waffen-SS men at some distance up the street. They had stopped a soldier who was alone and they seemed to be interrogating him. Since their backs were turned, they had not seen us.

Our lieutenant sharply ordered in a hushed voice, 'Quick, hide behind this building.'

We slipped out of sight into a narrow alleyway. There was a low wall we could just put our heads over. As we watched from behind the wall we saw the SS men grab the soldier, a young kid, and start shoving him. One of them held him and the other pulled his arms behind his back and tied his hands with a rope. Once he had tied the lad's hands he produced another rope, this one much longer. We could tell they were yelling at the kid, but we couldn't make out what they were saying. It was obvious what was going to happen. Maybe these two had orders to round up all the 'deserters', and the chances were they were the men who had hanged the soldier in the previous town.

We were all armed with our *Sturmgewehre* and had our pistols in our holsters.

Our lieutenant looked at us and said almost in a whisper, 'All of you, come with me. We are going to shoot these bastards. I am going to step out and I am going to confront them. Follow closely behind me. As soon as you see me aim my gun at them, you shoot.'

We nodded in silent acknowledgment.

Without hesitation, he walked out on the street, and we followed. He approached the SS at a brisk pace. They still didn't notice us until we got pretty close, as they had their backs turned and were so busy with their evil business.

'Hey, you, arseholes. Look at me!' our lieutenant shouted. He raised his gun as he spoke.

The SS men wheeled around, and as they were turning, the lieutenant took aim and shot the one closest to him. The other did not have the chance to raise his weapon before we shot him. Acting without hesitation, we had taken them completely by surprise.

We had killed a couple of SS. It was just too much to take. We had seen atrocities beyond description, we had been forced to witness and to be actors in senseless violence, and at this point, seeing the firepower that was relentlessly battering our bedraggled forces from the air and on the ground, we no longer harboured any hope for our country. We couldn't fathom what our future might be; I could not even imagine one. The enemy seemed determined to raze Germany to the ground. Airstrikes were constant now; several times a day we could see the American Thunderbolts and British Spitfires flying low, en route to hit another target. The only thing my pals and I could think of is that our families might all be buried under rubble, that we might have lost everything. And then to see our comrades in arms being murdered by our own forces in repayment for their service in defence of our country, when their only sin was to have accidentally survived the impossible, was an insult too unjust to bear.

Chapter 19

The Barbed Wire Incident

It was mid-morning on 7 May 1945. We were approaching Liezen. The road was busy with slow-moving traffic in front of us. We were in a convoy of a few personnel carriers, trucks with bench seats along each side. The tarpaulin covers were rolled up as it was warm.

In every personnel carrier there was an *Ausgucksmann*, a lookout man, a soldier ordered to watch the sky with field binoculars to advise the driver and the lieutenant if any planes were coming. That day it was my turn. I was intently scanning the clouds for any hint of movement, praying I wouldn't miss anything, painfully aware of the grave responsibility that lay on my shoulders. Suddenly I spotted Allied fighter-bombers.

'*Achtung*!' I yelled. 'All men out of the vehicle!'

We were in deadly danger, as the trucks on the road were an obvious target for enemy fire.

There was a fenced meadow right in front of us. Everybody jumped out of the trucks and started crawling flat on their bellies under the fence, to get as far away from the trucks and the road as possible. We were in full uniform, but as there were almost no supplies of anything left in those days, we had not been issued the standard green army dress; instead, we were wearing the uniform of General Rommel's Afrika Korps which was a light brown colour suitable for desert regions but highly visible in a bright green meadow. My truck was closest to the fence, so close that I thought I might be able to jump over the barbed wire rather than crawl under it. Since I was the *Ausguckmann*, always the last to be allowed to save himself, I waited nervously until everybody had got off and then awkwardly and hurriedly jumped off the back platform of the truck feet first in an attempt to clear the fence and land in the meadow. My jump was a little short, my bottom got snagged in the barbed wire and the seat of my trousers and underwear remained hanging on the spikes, like a yellowish flag flapping in the wind.

Everybody was down, arms over their helmets, listening to the deep drone of the bombers overhead, waiting. I was struggling to slow the pounding in my chest, not daring to look up for fear of what I might see. Luckily, the aim of the Allied planes wasn't very precise, and their bombs missed us by a long shot. They flew over us and dropped their load beyond the trees, perhaps all the while targeting something more important. As soon as the planes disappeared beyond the forest, we climbed to our feet. I could breathe again. We had had a lucky break, but occurrences like this had become a part of our daily reality. We silently accepted that we were still standing, until the next incident. What was the point of getting excited? Our lieutenant took a head count, and we got back into our trucks to continue our drive to Liezen.

Liezen was a sleepy little town tucked in a deep valley in the middle of Austria, surrounded by green fields that looked well-tended. It had not been bombed. Its onion-shaped church tower greeted us as we drove in, giving a false impression of peace. We drove into town, our short caravan crossing a bridge over the River Enns in a northbound direction, without any fanfare. Nobody greeted us, waved flags or shouted, 'Heil Hitler!', and yet, although nobody cheered or celebrated, it was a momentous event. We had made it across the demarcation line. We might live to see the end after all. Our relief manifested itself as overwhelming fatigue, as the adrenaline that had been fuelling us dissolved.

Once we arrived we went into private quarters, which meant that we were put up in civilian homes for however long our stay might last. With my bare bum, I wasn't overly keen to show up at a private residence, but we stopped in front of a house, our lieutenant knocked, and a middle-aged woman wearing the apron dirndl dress typical of the region opened the door. The lieutenant took her aside and spoke to her.

'Could you please look, this one has had a mishap with his trousers,' he said, pointing to me.

I wanted the earth to swallow me whole; I could feel my cheeks flaring brighter than my carrot-coloured hair.

The woman raised her eyebrows, slightly amused, looked at me and just said, 'Well, come on in, young man.'

I had no choice but to follow her into the house, crossing my arms behind my back in a vain attempt to cover my backside with my hands. I could have sworn I heard chuckling behind me as I walked inside.

The woman gave me a pair of trousers that belonged to her husband, who was away somewhere in the war. The trousers went well with the jacket I had on, my tan-coloured jacket from the Afrika Korps, and that made me feel better. She was a nice woman, comfortable-looking, who reminded me of my many aunts. She seemed a little sad but she tried to make me feel at home as best she could. She made me dinner and a cup of coffee, which was an unheard-of luxury. This was a valuable commodity she must have been saving for a special occasion, or more likely to trade in when the need arose. Instead, she gave it to me. I was, of course, a German soldier, and any civilian had a duty to harbour soldiers in the war, but I think the woman saw that perhaps I was a little young to be wearing uniform and took pity on me. Somehow, she still cared.

I didn't mind her pampering me a little. My mind wandered, and I felt that if I just closed my eyes I would be back at home again in my mother's dining room, where she and the aunts were having a comfortable *Kaffeeklatsch*, an afternoon chat over coffee, complete with delicious homemade cake, while my cousins and I were having fun playing football, breathlessly chasing each other out in the back garden in the crisp afternoon breeze, before all these horrible things happened.

'Pass the ball, Willi,' my little cousin Paule yelled, running alongside me, trying to get my attention while we were being chased by his big brother, cousin Yüppi, who was in the opposing team and determined not to let us score.

I laughed, running faster, 'I've got this, Paule. Don't worry, we'll kick their arses.'

I was smiling to myself when a voice jolted me out of my daydream back into reality.

'So, where are you from, soldier?' the lady of the house asked as we sat at the dinner table.

'Witten an der Ruhr, Westphalia.'

'Ah, that's far away.' She paused. 'Do you miss your family?'

'Yes,' I admitted quietly. 'Yes, I do.'

She sipped her coffee thoughtfully. 'We all miss someone these days, don't we?'

The cuckoo clock on the wall chirped, announcing the top of the hour, and then all was quiet again but for the ticking away of the minutes and the slight clink of my spoon against the bowl as I ate. She sighed, her hands folded on her apron.

'I miss my Hermann. Haven't heard from him in a while.'

I looked down at my bowl, not knowing what to say.

'Perhaps we'll all see our families again soon,' she added, in a vague attempt to dispel the awkward silence.

'Yes,' I offered. 'Perhaps.'

I appreciated her generosity, and the simple warm meal of potato and beet stew felt like the best I'd ever had. As the food settled in my belly and filled me with warmth, I realized I didn't remember the last time I'd had a home-cooked meal. What I didn't realize that evening was how long it would be until I had another one.

Chapter 20

The Ceasefire

It was 8 May 1945. I had spent the night at the lady's house where my lieutenant had dropped me off. Early in the morning, a soldier from the unit did the rounds, calling everybody out of their quarters to go to shooting practice.

'*Komm schon*, let's go,' he rushed me. 'I've got other people to go get.'

I scrambled to grab my jacket and Rucksack, said goodbye to the lady, and we were off. Along the way, the soldier picked up a couple of other chaps and marched us to where our trucks were parked, where others were already waiting. We drove to a nearby meadow, parked, lined up to get our gear out of the truck, set up targets and practised shooting with our pistols and our *Sturmgewehre*. It didn't seem to make a lot of sense, considering we were trying to give ourselves up, but that is what we did. Order and discipline had to be maintained, maybe even more so now that we were in retreat; it was important to stop us giving in to fear and confusion, which is why they wanted to keep us busy. We must have been at it for two or three hours when they told us we were finished.

When we got back into town, the lieutenant gave the unit a break. We got off our trucks dressed in full battle gear, as we had not taken it off at the end of shooting practice. I had my steel helmet on, the *Sturmgewehr* slung over my shoulder, a *Panzerfaust* hanging from my belt and my pistol in its holster. It was just about midday, and the sun felt hot with all my gear on, but we all kept it on, as much because we had not been told to take it off as because we didn't really want to. Maybe we felt safe in it. As we were standing around joking and carrying on we attracted the curiosity of the locals, mostly women, kids and old men. Some women approached and started talking to us.

'*Grüss Gott*, soldier,' said a smiling young woman, probably in her early twenties. Her hair was blonde and her eyes were a sparkling clear blue like a pool of fresh water. She was so beautiful that I could not take my eyes off her.

'*Grüss Gott, Fräulein*,' I replied, grinning rather sheepishly.

'Would you like me to show you around?'

'Well, yes, I would like that very much.'

I had no idea how I, of all the guys, had got so lucky, but I didn't really know what else to do, other than just go for a walk dressed in my battle gear with this pretty woman who was much older than me. She wanted to show me the centre of town, and who was I to turn her down? Why not enjoy her company on this beautiful spring day, no questions asked? I stood up a little straighter and felt a whole head taller, smugly taking in the jealous glances my comrades were shooting at me. My chest felt like it was going to burst with pride. *She picked me. She picked me out of the whole bunch. Yess!*

What we did not know that morning was that Grand Admiral Dönitz, the man in charge since the Führer had committed suicide on 1 May, had authorized Generaloberst Alfred Jodl, the Chief of Operations Staff of the Armed Forces High Command, to meet with the Allies and sign the unconditional surrender of the German forces on 7 May at 2301 Central European Time. This meant the war had effectively ended at midnight.

Here I was walking with this young woman at noon on 8 May, ignorant of what just happened. She was making small talk, all the while trying to get a better look at my face, which was partially obscured by an ill-fitting steel helmet that fell almost over my eyes because it was too big for me. I noticed a slight shift in her tone.

'Do you miss your mum?' she asked

'Not really,' I muttered.

Her question annoyed me because I was not a little boy any more, but I guess she had finally got a good look at me and realized I was a lot younger than she had thought.

'I was in a lot of dangerous battles pushing back the Bolsheviks,' I bragged.

'*Na Junge*, we have a beautiful and quiet town here. Don't you worry about that right now,' she replied in a soothing tone of voice.

I don't need mothering. What does she think she's doing? Doesn't she realize I am a soldier of the Reich?

We were approaching the town centre while she prattled on about something. I was not listening and looking at the ground, preoccupied by my annoyance with her. As we turned the sharp corner into the open square, I glanced up and froze.

Parked right there in the centre of the marketplace was a Jeep with four American soldiers in it. They had set up a *Vierlingsflak* on the jeep, four machine guns, each pointing in a different direction, one man per gun. In a matter of seconds they saw me, standing there in my steel helmet, fully armed, in the middle of the street with a young woman next to me.

I never threatened them. I did not pick up my *Sturmgewehr*. I did nothing. They were acting like you saw in the movies, leaning back and sunning themselves with their legs up on the sides of the truck. They were wearing rubber boots, strange things I had never seen before, and the light was hitting them at an angle that made it reflect off them. The Americans stared blankly at me for what seemed a long moment, then suddenly, to a man, they leapt into action. The engine revved, tyres screeched and, leaving skid marks on the old town square, they sped off as fast as their Jeep would carry them. My hand had slid to my *Sturmgewehr*, because if they started to shoot, I would have had to shoot back. But nothing had happened. They just took off. I immediately turned on my heel and ran back at full speed to my unit, leaving the poor woman standing in the square.

Willi's grandparents' golden wedding celebration, 1934.

The Jewish ancestor's trunk.

The ancestral village of Delbrück.

Willi with his cone of sweets on his first day of school, aged six, 1936.

Sitting on a trunk on his first day of school, 1936.

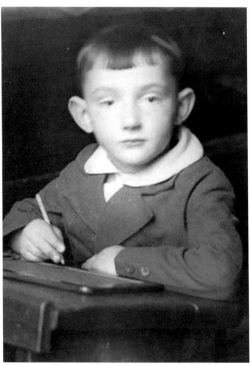
Willi at his desk in first grade.

Willi, aged eight, in the family living room with his parents, 1938.

Text und Bild aus Deutsches Lesebuch für Volksschulen,
Bd. 2, Dortmund 1941 (4. Auflage), S. 272 u. 273

RMfWEV v. 21. 12. 40: Die Jungen und Mädel des Jahrgangs 1930/31, die in der Zeit vom 1. Juli 1930 bis 30. Juni 1931 geboren sind, werden demnächst auf Grund des Gesetzes über die Hitler-Jugend . . . aufgerufen werden. Ich bin damit einverstanden, daß die Schulen . . . bei der Aufstellung der Erfassungslisten mitwirken.

Meine Erfassung war also geschehen. Die Volksschule meldete mich. Ich erhielt eine Einladung zur Prüfung.

Hitlers Lebenslauf natürlich, die Wessel-Hymne, das Deutschland-Lied, irgendwelche anderen Texte . . . Trotz gewisser Beklemmungen waren alle angenommen, die da in einer seltsamen Konkurrenzstimmung sich getroffen hatten. Nun hieß es, die Kluft kaufen, den Knoten, das Braunhemd, Fahrtenmesser und Feldflasche usw.

Mein Vater – entweder Parteibeitritt oder entsprechende Folgen für einen Beamten und seine Familie! – hielt still, kaufte, duldete. Vielleicht erduldete er auch, wenn ich an den Verlauf des Krieges und seine Folgen für meine Familie denke.

Willi's schoolbook.

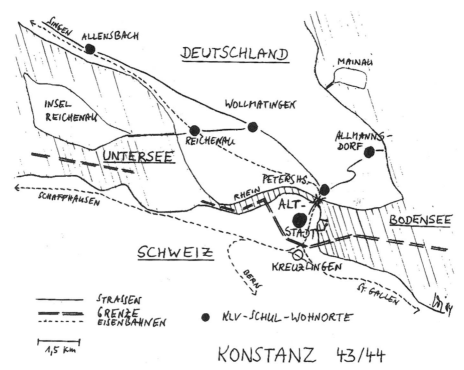

A sketch of Konstanz. KLV living quarters and school locations marked with a black dot. (Gerhard Wiehe, *Penne 41–51*)

Lunch at the KLV (*Kinderlandverschickung*): Willi, back left, in the Konstanz dining room with a representative of the NSV (National Socialist Association) standing behind him, and a teacher sitting down to his left. Picture of a Nazi officer in background. Representatives of the KLV were the students' handlers, responsible for their supervision at all times. (Gerhard Wiehe, *Penne 41–51*)

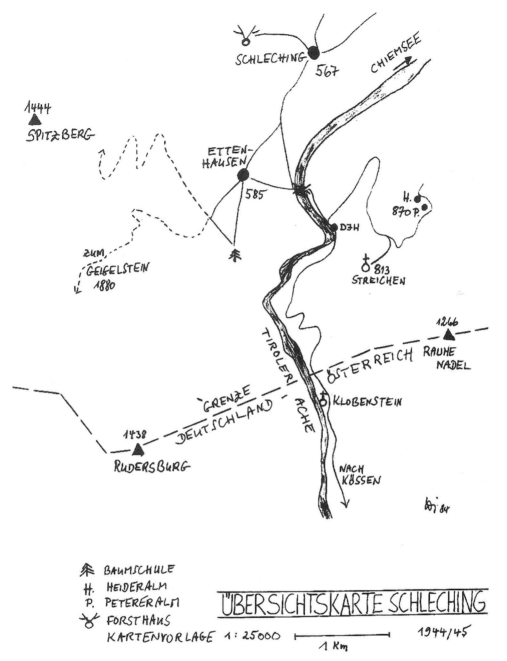

A sketch of Schleching. (Gerhard Wiehe, *Penne 41-51*)

The Vollmar family's farewell postcard to Willi, December 1944: Lake Konstanz.

The postcard's message: 'Farewell to our Hans-Willi!'

Willi with his parents, 1943.

Hotel Zur Post, Schleching. (Gerhard Wiehe, *Penne 41–51*)

T-34 tank. (The Taylor Library)

A soldier in a foxhole holding a *Panzerfaust*.

Discharged by the Area Control Commission (US) from the First German Army at EBERSBERG vor München, Bavaria.

C. V. CLIFTON
Lt. Col. FA
Commanding

Control Form D.2
Kontroll-Form D.2

Certificate of Discharge
Entlassungsschein

All entries will be made in block Latin Capitals and will be made in ink or Type Script.
Alle Eintragungen sind in grossen lateinischen Anfangsbuchstaben vorzunehmen. Tinte oder Schreibmaschine benützen.

Personal ~~Particulars~~
Persönliche Angaben

Surname of Holder / Zuname des Inhabers: **LANGBEIN**

Date of Birth / Geburtsdaten: **12. MAI 1930**
Day / Tag — Month / Monat — Year / Jahr

Christian Name / Vorname: **WILLI**

Place of Birth / Geburtsort: **WITTEN**

Civil Occupation / Zivilberuf: **SCHÜLER UND LANDWIRT**

Family Status / Stand: Single† / Ledig
~~Married / Verheiratet~~
~~Widow (er) / Witwe (r)~~
~~Divorced / Geschieden~~

Home Address / Wohnadresse: **WITTEN / RUHR JOHANNISSTRASSE 25**

Number of children who are minors / Anzahl der minderjährigen Kinder: **KEINE**

I hereby certify that to the best of my knowledge and belief the particulars given above are true.
Ich bestätige nach bestem Wissen und Gewissen, dass die obigen Angaben wahr sind.

I also certify that I have read and understood the "Instructions to Personnel on Discharge" (Control Form D.1).
Ich bestätige weiter, dass ich die „Anweisungen an das Personal bei Entlassung" (Kontroll-Form D.1) gelesen und verstanden habe.

Signature of Holder / Unterschrift des Inhabers

Name of Holder in Block Latin Capitals: **WILLI LANGBEIN**
Name des Inhabers in grossen lateinischen Anfangsbuchstaben

† Delete that which is inapplicable.
Nichtzutreffendes durchstreichen.

Willi's *Entlassungsschein* (Certificate of Discharge) from the German Army, Kirchseeon Separation Center, 1945 (front).

Medical Certificate
Ärztliches Gutachten

Distinguishing Marks...... Brillenträger
Besondere Kennzeichen

Disability, with Description ...... keine
Untauglichkeit (beschreiben)

Medical Category ...... arbeitsfähig
Ärztliche Klassifizierung

I certify that to the best of my knowledge and belief the above particulars relating to the holder are true and that he is not verminous or suffering from any infectious or contagious disease.

Ich bestätige nach bestem Wissen und Gewissen, dass die sich auf den Inhaber beziehenden, obigen Angaben wahr sind und dass er frei von Ungeziefer und ansteckenden Krankheiten ist.

Signature of Medical Officer ......
Unterschrift des Militärarztes

Name and Rank of Medical Officer ...... Stabsarzt SCHULTE
Name und Dienstgrad des Militärarztes   In Block Latin Capitals
                                              In grossen lateinischen Anfangsbuchstaben

II

The person to whom the above particulars refer was discharged on ...... 15. JUNE 1945
Die Person, auf die sich obige Angaben   (Date of Discharge)
beziehen, wurde entlassen am   (Datum der Entlassung)

From the° ...... WEHRMACHT / HEER
Von der (dem)

Right Thumbprint   Official Impressed Seal
Rechter   Offizieller
Daumenabdruck   Stempel

° Insert Army, Navy, Air Force, Volkssturm or Para-Military Organization, e.g. "RAD", "NSFK", etc.

Hier ist Armee, Kriegsmarine, Luftwaffe oder halbmilitärische Verbände, wie Reichsarbeitsdienst, Nationalsozialistisches Fliegerkorps usw. einzusetzen.

Certified by ...... FA
Beglaubigt durch

Name, rank and appointment of Allied Discharging Officer ...... PAUL M. FRANK   CAPTAIN   FA
Name, Dienstgrad und   In Block Latin Capitals
Titel des entlassenden   In grossen lateinischen
Offiziers.   Anfangsbuchstaben.

KIRCHSEEON SEPARATION CENTER

Certificate of Discharge (back).

Willi at the farm (standing, far left) wearing his *Afrika Korps* jacket.

Willi's portrait, aged sixteen, 1946.

Witten in 1945 before the bombing.

Witten in 1945 after the bombing.

Johannisstrasse 25, the family house under construction after the war.

Willi as goalkeeper, 1951.

Willi (second from left), aged twenty-one, in the schoolyard at break, senior year, 1951.

Engagement photograph, 1957. (L to R) Willi's mother Maria, Willi's father Joseph, fiancée Teresa, Willi, Teresa's mother Amparo.

Willi and Teresa, just engaged.

Willi in his late thirties.

Medal of European Merit Certificate, 1979.

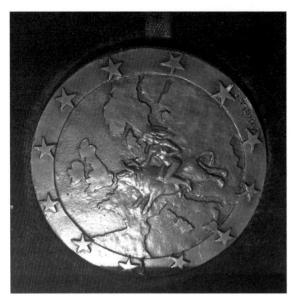
Medal of European Merit.

The author with her father, Willi, aged eighty-four, 2014.

I spotted the lieutenant on the street standing by the trucks and shouted, out of breath, 'Sir, I have seen the Amis, they ran away from me!'

He shouted back, 'For God's sake, Langbein, I have just heard on the radio that we have a cease-fire!' Germany has capitulated!

I stopped dead in my tracks. Sweat was trickling down my back and my heavy gear was weighing me down – so critical just a minute ago, those words had suddenly rendered it utterly unnecessary. One moment we were killing each other because we were told to, and the next it was over because somebody said so, just like that. I had witnessed people being slaughtered, I had shot people, my comrades had been blown up. And now? The enormity of those words had punched me in the stomach. I could not move my legs; I was becoming dizzy. Overwhelming relief at being alive, at having beaten the odds and maybe finally being able to go home, mingled with the realization of defeat and a creeping apprehension. What was going to happen to us? Slowly, my awareness returned to my surroundings, and I saw that there was pandemonium around me. The lieutenant and the other officers were shouting over each other, trying to reconfirm the news on their radios, news that was spreading like wildfire among our unit and the town. Some people were running, some just sitting on the ground holding their heads. A few were softly crying, whether from grief or happiness I couldn't tell.

The lieutenant finally made contact with other dispersed units of our division over a two-way radio, in an attempt to locate everybody and spread the news. It was then that I found out what unit I had been fighting in. We were the first division of the First German Army Corps at Ebersberg in Bavaria. This information later appeared on my discharge papers, my US Certificate of Discharge. I never knew this until that point. Since I hadn't exactly joined or been drafted in any official way, a lot of formalities had been skipped. I had just been loaded on to a truck with my pals Helmut and Knapsack back on that mountain and driven to the front. It started to dawn on me that nobody had really expected us to survive – so why waste time giving unnecessary information to some kids?

Our division had decided to give themselves up to the Americans somewhere. I don't know how, but they had contacted the Americans and it was arranged we would surrender to them at an agreed location. There was a small river called the Lamme nearby, and somewhere along it was a very large meadow, which was exactly the right size to accommodate the division, or what was left of us. No longer a division of several thousand men, we had shrunk to a small outfit, maybe around a hundred of us. We settled in this meadow beside the river and waited for the Americans to come and take us prisoner.

We waited there a couple of days, but nothing happened. The first day, everybody was concerned with settling in and absorbing the news of the surrender. Men found a patch of grass to call their own, most trying to stay close to the parked trucks, and put down what little they had on some surface to keep it off the damp grass. The second day, absolutely nothing happened other than waiting, which made the hours crawl by at a snail's pace. Hunger was setting in as there was no food at all. Boredom was making people restless and irritable; they argued over unimportant things like who had a better spot or a bigger blanket. I mostly tried to keep to myself, lacking the energy to get into any discussions.

Then, on 12 May 1945, the third day in the meadow, my birthday came around. I turned fifteen years old. Not a lot was going on, and we mostly slept because we were weak from lack of food. I thought of my last birthday in Konstanz with the Vollmar family, an eternity ago. That day, I had had a full belly from the delicious *Bündner Nusstorte* Frau Vollmar had baked, and my greatest troubles were that I missed my parents and that school was boring. I had just got my first suit with long trousers, marking my transition from boy to young man. Little did I know how brutal that transition would be. For lunch, on this birthday, we were told to cut the stems off the grass in the meadow which the division cook threw into a big pot with boiling water. He probably added a couple of Maggi brand bouillon cubes, and somehow it tasted OK. But it wasn't anything that could fill you up. We had no bread, no potatoes, nothing. When we had finished the soup, a pal of mine offered me a drag of his cigarette. Up to now I had resisted the temptation to smoke, remembering my parents' warnings of the evils of tobacco, but this time I accepted it, not having anything better to do, and was surprised to find that it made me lightheaded, and not in a bad way. That is when I took up smoking. The real benefit of it, my pal taught me, was that nicotine kills your appetite; that was obviously a good thing for us, since we didn't have any food.

It so happened that I had a big store of cigarettes in my pack. On our way to Liezen, as we were retreating from the Russians, we had come across a Wehrmacht supply depot. Our lieutenant had ordered us to stop the trucks.

'We're going to go in there to get some supplies, boys.'

We pushed the door open with our guns drawn, shouting, 'Come on, hand over the provisions!'

An *Oberfeldwebel*, a sergeant, who was guarding the place, yelled, 'Hey, you can't just come in here! Where are your orders?'

Our lieutenant spat back, 'You can kiss my arse with your orders! Hand over the goods.'

We rushed in. I grabbed several cartons of cigarettes that I shoved into my pack as best as I could, together with some things to eat, and ran out. I meant to save those cigarettes all the way home to Witten for my family, because I knew that with them we could buy things on the black market, food and other necessities, since cigarettes had become a valuable currency.

Back in the meadow, the next day, 13 May, I managed to sneak into a truck and went to sleep on top of a pile of brown SA uniforms that provided some padding. While I was sleeping, the division received a shipment of provisions, and everybody got fed. It was a kind of south Bavarian casserole, *Auflauf*. At some point I woke up and, as I jumped off the truck, I saw my pals walking in my direction.

'Willi, where were you? We looked for you and we couldn't find you. You haven't had a helping of this stuff they're serving? We've had thirds already.'

Oh, hell, no … My stomach sank to my feet with a sense of cold foreboding. I broke into a run with what little energy I could still muster. When I got within sight of the cook I could tell it was all gone, because he was cleaning out the pots.

He saw me coming and shrugged his shoulders.

'Too late, my friend.'

'Oh, mate, this can't be happening. Don't you have anything?'

I must have sounded rather pitiful because he started rummaging around the pots and pans, found a couple of biscuits that were left over and handed them to me. Feeling sorry for myself, I shoved them into my mouth. I wanted to cry, as much from sadness and hunger as from frustration. It wasn't fair, none of this was fair. The things that were happening to me, I hadn't asked for any of them. This horrible war had destroyed everything; I just wanted to be home with my family and friends and go to school like I was supposed to. Why couldn't I just do that? I wished for the hundredth time it was all a bad dream that I could shake off. But there I was, sitting on wet grass waiting to be taken prisoner, biting back tears and holding in my very real stomach cramps.

The man in charge of our division was only an *Oberst*, a Colonel. A division should have been the command of a General, specifically of a *Generalmajor* according to German regulations of the time. But there was no General around, and the next-highest ranking officer left was the *Oberst*. His last name was Bayer.

That afternoon, *Oberst* Bayer told us, 'We have to set up a night patrol. The Amis aren't here yet, and we have to see to it that we protect the German soldiers who try to flee. We must protect them from the SS, who will shoot them on sight. Your job is to keep our

German comrades in our camp so we can all give ourselves up to the Amis.'

We kept watch throughout the night, but a couple of soldiers ran away while I was on duty. The orders were that if they ran we were to shoot them, which was completely ridiculous. I didn't even consider doing it. The absurdity of having to shoot somebody so they wouldn't get shot by somebody else couldn't possibly be escaping everybody – or could it?

Someone told the *Oberst* the next day that I had let the soldiers go and didn't shoot at them, and he called me to his tent.

'What's your name?' he asked me.

'Langbein.'

I stiffened.

'Where are you from?'

'I hail from Witten an der Ruhr, sir.'

'So, you have not followed my order to shoot at soldiers trying to escape?'

I braced myself, lifting my chin.

'I know that, but I will not shoot at German soldiers.'

He looked intently at me for a moment, the corners of his mouth turned down in disdain, and then he said, 'You know, I am not surprised that we have lost the war with idiots like you taking part.'

That was a bit much for a kid who had just turned fifteen. With the wind knocked out of me, I turned on my heels without a word, walked back numbly to the truck, put my stuff up and went to sleep.

Chapter 21

The Internment Camp

The radio control post of our tank-hunter division was abuzz with activity. We had finally managed to made contact with the German Army Corps and we transmitted our exact coordinates to them so that the Americans could finally get busy and take us prisoner. We had had enough of waiting around in that meadow.

The soldiers had got bored and started fooling around. Some of them took their machine guns and pistols and fired them off into the woods, the trees or the river, because they had nothing better to do. One morning, the Americans, as was typical of them, reconnoitred our camp by flying some bombers and fighter planes over it to establish our exact location. We heard, then saw them overhead, the silhouettes and deep droning of the bombers deeply unnerving. Then they disappeared, but it wasn't too long before they returned.

A couple of days after that fly-by the American troops finally showed up again, for good this time, and we dutifully raised our hands, threw away our guns and sat down in their convoys. Initially I had tried to save my pistol, but before we got to the prison camp, the Kirchseeon separation centre near Munich, a fellow said to me, 'Willi, throw the pistol away. If the Amis find you with a gun they'll hang you from the nearest tree.'

I looked at the pistol with regret. There is a powerful connection between a soldier and his weapon; it can make the difference between life and death. This one had saved my life back in my first battle, and it meant a lot to me. I had wanted to take it home with me to Witten. But I knew the guy was right, so I threw it away. It landed somewhere in the fields, left to rust away there like so many other remnants of the war that would litter the landscape, ghostly reminders of what had happened.

Since the war had officially ended, we entered captivity under the Allied forces not as prisoners of war but as 'interned persons'; you can only take prisoners of war during a war, not after it is over. It was an awkward intermediate position: we were prisoners but weren't called prisoners. It seemed as if we were stuck in a grey area, and they didn't quite know what to do with us. We were a problem that they would rather not have had to deal with.

The Amis had organized the camp in Kirchseeon in a large open field fenced in with barbed wire and with floodlights, outfitted with latrines and other structures but with no barracks for the prisoners. There were troughs of cold water where we could drink and wash. We slept in the open on thin blankets we had been issued. Luckily, it was late spring and warm. We were also issued a tin bowl and a US Armed Forces spoon, with 'U.S.' engraved on its handle, but there was scarcely any food for us on which to use these utensils. On most days we lined up once a day for a bowl of thin soup and a slice of mouldy bread. This made a lot of men sick, and many died. I don't think anybody cared how many of us died; probably the more the better, they thought.

The Americans might not have cared if we died, but apparently they cared that we did so while clean. They were mad on hygiene, so sometime after we were processed into the camp we were told to line up out in the field to be de-loused.

'Everybody, take all of your clothes off and leave them here. When you are done, march to the de-lousing station over there.'

A soldier was pointing with his rifle to where they wanted us to go. We did as they said, but I stripped off my clothes and attempted to fold them rather than just dropping them on the ground.

'Come on, you, move along, move along!' The soldier came close and pointed his rifle at me.

I moved. I lined up with a bunch of other chaps, feeling cold despite the warm weather. As I got to the front of the line, my turn came.

They barked, 'Step forward. Stand still. Arms up.'

A startling blast of white powder hit me from a spray gun, mostly aimed at my underarms and my private parts but getting all over my face and the rest of my body, making my eyes burn and leaving a nasty taste in my mouth.

'Move aside! Move!' I heard.

I stumbled out of the way. It was a deeply humiliating experience. We were treated like vermin. I could feel in the looks of disdain they gave us that this was what they thought we were. It was very disconcerting to me. I knew we had lost the war, but they seemed to despise us deeply, and from my limited perspective I could not really understand why. Nonetheless, I just had to accept the fact that this was the way it was.

The soldiers who watched us were Blacks. They were not so bad as they, unlike the white soldiers, showed us some sympathy and treated us like human beings. As it happened, I spoke a bit of English and was able to communicate with them. They told me, in their thick American accents, that they knew what it was like to be treated badly. I didn't understand everything they were saying, but I did get the gist of it. And they gave us cigarettes, which I gratefully accepted although I had enough cigarettes of my own, because I had managed to hang on to my pack. This interaction was somewhat of a revelation for us, who had never seen or talked to black people. We had been told they were inferior, but they seemed perfectly fine to me. Like other details I had started noticing, reality did not always seem to fit what we had been told.

Word had got out that I was the only one in the camp who spoke any English, the little I had learned in school and had retained because I had a good ear for languages. An American Captain named Frank called me to his barracks, a makeshift prefabricated building. He was sitting behind a desk, and I could see an open door behind him that led to what looked like a bedroom.

'Do you speak English, soldier?'

'I ... a little,' I stammered.

'Then stand here against this wall. Lift up your hands and stay there.'

He pointed to the bedroom.

'My German girlfriend is coming, and you are going to translate for me what she says.'

I could do nothing but follow his orders. Frank had evidently decided it would be amusing to torment me, so he had sex with the German girl in front of me, and I had to translate the things she said. I stared at the ground because I couldn't bear to watch. My Catholic upbringing had been very strict, and I was horrified at what was going on. I thought of my mother and how disgusted she would be. I prayed to God to make it stop. This was a terrible sin. Burning shame overwhelmed me, making my skin crawl. I felt soiled. At some point I just couldn't take it anymore. I lowered my arms and simply left the room.

Frank, naked as he was, came running after me with his gun in his hand, and yelled, 'Hands in the air, NOW,' in perfect German, so I slowly turned and lifted my hands back up. At that point I had made my mind up that I wasn't going back in there again.

I looked him in the eyes and said, 'Looks like you speak German better than me.'

He answered in German, 'That is the revenge we are taking on the German people.'

I stared at him, bewildered. I didn't know what he was talking about. And then I saw it. The pendant around his neck was the Star of David. The image of the burnt-down synagogue in Witten that morning on my way to school when I was eight years old shot into my head. I had known then that things were not all right, and I had felt a sick feeling in my stomach. This man was spitting in my face, eyes bulging, channelling tremendous hatred at me I could feel in every fibre of my body. The intensity of his rage physically pushed me back. Something was horribly wrong, and he was taking it out on me. That same sick feeling came back.

It was not over for me. I was going to be punished for my impertinence. Frank, a German Jew who had emigrated to America, was in the CIA, so after he had hastily put on his trousers he took me to other officers in the camp. He told them something in a hushed tone of voice and left me with them. They led me into a room that had been converted into an office, with a desk, a typewriter and a chair. There were four men in the room who said they wanted to know how it came to be that a kid as young as I was a soldier in the German Army.

'The only explanation is that you are a devout Nazi, so young. I bet you couldn't wait to volunteer, you little scum. Did your daddy work in a concentration camp? Did he enjoy torturing Jews? Huh? Say it!'

I looked at him in utter confusion. *What is he talking about?*

'You Nazi vermin have to be exterminated!' one of them shouted in my face, so close I could feel his hot breath and the spittle spraying my face.

As he shouted, he punched me in the stomach so hard it knocked the wind out of me. Then they all proceeded to beat me up. They pummelled me to the ground and kicked and punched me repeatedly in the head until the blood in my eyes blinded me, and kicked my private parts so hard the pain was unbearable. I moaned and curled up in a ball trying to protect myself, but they kept pulling my arms and legs back so they could better aim their kicks at the soft parts of my body. I was spitting blood, my ears were ringing, I could not breathe any more, but they continued to beat me until I finally lost consciousness, and they left me there on the ground, perhaps for dead.

I woke up in the sickbay, I think it was the next day. My private parts were swollen to the size of a melon. The pain was so excruciating I could not move. My eyes were swollen shut, and I was very thirsty, but nobody was there to give me water. Some of my ribs were broken, and my ears felt like there was cotton wool in them. There were several other sick soldiers there, but I couldn't make anything out, because I was so dizzy and blind. There was a German state physician there who treated me. His name was Schulte, and as it turned out he was the one who eventually signed my release from the internment camp. He was matter of fact, unemotional. I don't think he was really capable of showing emotion anymore, and I didn't expect it.

When I got out of the sickbay several days later I was still barely able to walk, because my private parts had been so gravely injured. I told my fellow inmates what happened. They were simply happy to find I was still alive. Nobody had told them where I was, and when people disappeared they usually didn't come back. So I suppose I was lucky, although it didn't really feel that way.

At some point the American soldiers came round and showed us gruesome pictures of what they said were concentration camps, death camps set up by the Nazis to exterminate the Jewish people.

'Here, take a good look. This is what you people have done. Every one of you is guilty of these murders. You don't deserve any mercy. You should all be starved to death, like you did to them. Too bad we are not allowed to do that.'

We were aghast at what we saw in those dreadful images. They didn't make sense. It could not be. The people at home, they were good people. I had been told the Reich was being attacked by the enemy and we were defending ourselves. There had to be some other explanation. But then, the creeping suspicion surfaced again. I remembered the yellow stars the Jews had to wear on their sleeves. And when I overheard Papa say to Mama that she couldn't shop at Herr Rosenbaum's shoe shop any more or it would cause us trouble.

I remembered talk that Jews were bad people, and that I couldn't understand why, on account of Herr Rosenbaum being so nice. Could it be that we were the monsters they said we were? No, they had to be lies. Nothing made sense any more. The world around me was collapsing, and I was falling into a dark, bottomless hole.

Chapter 22

The Long Road Home

The day of our release from the camp came without warning. It was the morning of 15 June 1945. We were ordered to gather any belongings we might have and line up to receive our *Entlassungsschein*, our Certificate of Discharge, from the Kirchseeon internment camp, or 'Separation Center' as the Americans called it.

As I stood in the long line carrying my only possession, my backpack containing my precious cigarettes which for some inexplicable reason I had been able to keep until now, I could overhear the questions the medical officer, Dr Schulte, was asking each prisoner standing in front on him, and could see him meticulously write down each answer he received on the certificate in front of him. When he was done he signed the certificate with his fountain pen, stamped it and fastidiously blotted the ink with a large half-moon-shaped wooden blotter, before handing it to the prisoner. He seemed fully absorbed in what he was doing, as if this repetitive task brought the comfort of some semblance of normality back into his life.

One of the questions he asked each prisoner was about his peacetime occupation. I quickly noticed that two lines were materializing in front of me. The men receiving their discharge papers were directed to one or the other by the doctor after answering some questions. I tried hard to home in on what they were saying and managed to hear that a couple of the guys who had answered that they were farmers were put in the same line, and guys that answered with another trade were placed in the other line. Suddenly, I had a flash of inspiration. *They're sending the farmers home.* That had to be it.

There was no reason to separate them out otherwise. This might be my chance to get home.

When it was my turn, Dr Schulte, who had overseen my care when I was recovering from the beating, asked me, without looking up from his paperwork:

'Name?'
'Wilhelm Langbein.'
'Date of birth?'
'12 May 1930.'

He shot me a quick glance, a glimmer of recognition in his eyes, then looked down again, and carefully wrote my birth date down. Then, he wrote in remarks *'Brillenträger'* – spectacles-wearer, which I was.

'Peacetime occupation?'
I swallowed hard.
'Student and farmer, sir.'

He looked at me again, a little longer this time, nodded almost imperceptibly and proceeded to carefully note down the information. He handed me the form, stamped and signed, and pointed to the line where the other farmers had been sent. I was fairly sure I was going home and the guys in the other line weren't. I felt almost giddy with relief. Maybe everything was going to be all right now.

As it turned out, we quickly discovered that the other guys were sent to labour camps in France to work in the mines. They were to return only much later, including my cousin Franz Bach, who had to work as a miner in the Alsace region of France and wasn't released until 1947.

Six days later, on 21 June, we were loaded on to trucks that drove us to the Kirchseeon station, where a dilapidated-looking goods train was waiting for us at the platform. The soldiers started shoving us into the wagons, cramming us in like herrings. These were open cattle trucks with no doors; the openings through which the farm animals, and now the prisoners, were loaded were secured by a chain across the width of the opening locked with a bolt on one side. As I was one of the last to be loaded on to the wagon, I ended up sitting at the opening along with other guys, holding on to the chain with my hands so as not to fall out, with my legs dangling out of the wagon. The others stood stacked behind us, pushing against us because the wagon was so full. Then the nightmare began.

We waited motionless at the deserted station for what seemed a long time, then the locomotive finally began to slowly pull away in the direction of Cologne-Düsseldorf. We had only covered a short distance before the train stopped and was switched to another track. This was to happen innumerable times during our long journey home. The train would also stop in the middle of nowhere for hours to let other trains pass. The Allies had bombed all the train tracks in Germany to cripple the transportation networks. When the American and British occupation began, they had tried to repair what tracks they could, but we still had to make crazy detours; we actually had to go through Belgium and continue across Holland to get back into Germany, since there was no other connection into the heavily bombed Ruhr region, my home. The trip from Munich to Düsseldorf that would have normally taken five hours lasted fourteen days.

Along the way, we encountered massive devastation on a scale I could not have imagined. The train moved slowly every time it reached a town, and time after time the same scene repeated itself: fire-blackened ruins, the remnants of pockmarked walls, collapsed buildings, kilometres-long mounds of bricks and rubble. It seemed impossible to me that anybody could have escaped alive. My sense of dread grew. Would anything, anybody still be there when I got home? I wanted to cry, but my eyes just ached in crusty dryness, unable to produce any more tears. I was staring in numb disbelief at the burned-out remains of my country, witness to the apocalyptic collapse of the German Reich, witness to the end of my world.

Inside the wagon, people were pressed against each other like sardines. There was no room to move. There was no food or drink. We urinated and defecated where we stood or sat, and we could not move, only crawl around a little if we were lucky. Some died where they stood, and the dead were pushed out of the wagon.

'Here comes another one,' I would hear behind me, announcing the dreadful passing of a body to the front.

This meant I would have to help in horror and disgust to shove yet another lifeless body off the car and watch it bounce like a rag doll off the hard, unforgiving ground that would be its only grave. Their families would never know what happened to them. They would be the 'missing'. *What would Mama and Papa do if I never got home? Would they look for me? But where?*

Occasionally a lukewarm *Essbecher*, a cup of thin soup, was handed to us by the American soldiers. It wasn't much, and I don't remember how often we got it, perhaps once every two days. That was the only food or drink we received for the duration of the trip. I just sat pressed against other bodies, motionless most of the time, having neither the ability nor the strength to do anything else. The fact that we were so tightly wedged against each other actually helped us to not slide off our precarious perch at the edge of the wagon into what would be our certain death. I was one of the lucky ones, because at least I wasn't suffocating in the back.

After a few days, time began to blur. Once more, the train stopped in the middle of an area of open fields, with no habitation in sight. We had halted for a train that was coming from the other direction carrying American soldiers, and it stopped, too. This was a slightly better transport, a passenger train. The American soldiers started jeering and hurling insults across at us, becoming loud and rowdy.

'Hey, you damn Krauts, not so arrogant any more, are we?'

It seemed like they were daring each other to do something. A sense of alarm registered in my brain, even though I could not hear what they were saying. I saw that a few of the soldiers, fully armed, had jumped out of their train and started coming toward us, with expressions that did not bode well. My spine tingled. I could not move. I could do nothing but watch them rapidly coming closer. They were laughing loudly and seemed to be taunting us, egging each other on in their thick American accents that I still had difficulty understanding.

One of them came right up to me and started waving his gun in my face. I shrank back a bit. He found it funny. I wished I hadn't flinched. He looked back at his comrades behind him who were hooting and hollering.

'Looks like this one's scared,' he gestured to his friends, pointing at me.

Then he turned back to look at me, grinned broadly and started to try to pull me out by my legs.

No, no, NO – I desperately tried to wriggle out of his grip, but my legs would not respond. I was trapped. My eyes swivelled to the guy next to me, and I grabbed his arm, but he just stared blankly back at me, all energy gone. He had nothing left to give, poor fellow.

Suddenly one of the soldiers who was guarding the train appeared from behind.

'Hey, you, stop!'

'What, you want to protect the Krauts? What's wrong with you? Get out of here!' the guy pulling my legs yelled back.

I was slowly losing my grip on the chain. I could feel my body slowly giving way and sliding off the wagon. I frantically tried to brace myself, gripping the chain with all the strength I had left. My body was teetering like a seesaw. Only my upper back still made any contact with the floor of the wagon, my arms wrapped around the chain pulled against my torso. The rest of my body dangled in mid-air.

'I told you to stop, you son of a bitch, that's an order!' the guard yelled.

The guy sneered. 'Whatever. Stop me if you can.'

Now the other soldiers who had jumped off the train got involved in defending their comrade, approaching our guard and arguing with him.

'Stop, or I swear I'll shoot you!' threatened the guard, pointing his gun at the soldier who was pulling my legs.

He didn't stop. A shot rang out. At that point, the soldier let me go and backed off, and they all started hastily retreating, because by then the commotion had attracted the attention of more guards. As they showed up, yelling 'Move back!' all the soldiers climbed back into their train. The guards remained standing in front of us in silent challenge until the other train finally started moving. In the meantime, I had managed to pull my way back into the wagon with the help of somebody who had hoisted me back up by grabbing me under the arms from behind. I shuddered. It was almost a miracle that I had made it. I was deeply grateful to the American guard, even though I knew he didn't do it for me.

Then the Dutch came. The train had continued its steady but halting path through Belgium and at some point crossed into Holland and passed the city of Roermond. The train stopped just outside of the city for no apparent reason, on a flat, soggy stretch of land. It appeared to be midday; a hazy sun was peering out from behind the clouds.

Suddenly a large crowd of people appeared out of nowhere with knives and guns in their hands. These people were Dutch *Wiederstandskämpfer*, resistance fighters. They were waving a communist flag with a hammer and sickle and chanting dark words I couldn't understand, but one thing was clear: they meant to get on the train and cut our throats. The enraged mob started howling and running toward us at top speed. The hate they exuded was palpable and it was directed at us. This realization terrified me. I knew then there would be no mercy from these people. Whatever the Germans had done to them, we were going to pay for it. We were sitting ducks; we could not defend ourselves. I could only sit there and watch it all unfold, almost detached despite the choking panic that had grabbed my throat and was not letting me breathe. So, this is how it ends, I thought in frozen dread and resignation, unable to take my eyes off the mesmerizing sight of this rapidly approaching mass of humanity, the dull sunlight reflecting off the blades they clutched as they came closer and closer, the rumbling noise of their voices and their trampling feet growing louder every second. *Oh God, please help us …*

Again, the American guards saved the day. They jumped out of the train further up front and started shooting while running in the direction of the crowd, not at the Dutchmen, but over their heads to make them go away. They kept shooting over the crowd, yelling at them to retreat.

'Get back, get back! Move or we'll shoot!' they shouted.

I think some did shoot into the crowd to make the message clear, as I saw people stumbling and tripping. From my perch, which gave me a front-row view, my knuckles white and numb from gripping the chain for dear life, I watched the crowd slowly and reluctantly retreating back in the direction they had come, hurling insults all the way. Rocks flew, more shots were fired. Eventually, the crowd dispersed. As I saw them leaving, a shiver shook my entire body. I could not believe I was still alive. *How many more times? Will we make it through the next one?*

Eventually, we approached the Ruhr valley, the heart of Germany's coal and steel industry in the region of Westphalia, where Düsseldorf and my home town of Witten were located. We passed densely forested hills and small villages in the distance that seemed to have been spared. But in fact this was one of the most heavily bombed regions of Germany. All the surrounding cities, Hagen, Wuppertal, Essen, Dortmund, had been repeatedly bombed and largely reduced to smoking piles of rubble. The train stopped at gutted stations along the way for no apparent reason; nobody got off or on.

The city of Düsseldorf, our final destination, had suffered the same fate. As we slowly approached the almost completely destroyed central station we saw the scarred remains of many structures. The buildings' gaping wounds exposed what once had been a kitchen or a living room, now senselessly suspended in mid-air. We smelled the acrid scent of burnt belongings that hung heavily in the atmosphere. We watched civilians and what looked like uniformed men rooting through the piles of debris as the train sighed and crawled along the tracks, metal wheels grinding and screeching, until we finally pulled in.

Since the wagon was secured with a chain, we had to wait until the guards came to unlock it and get us to wherever they were taking us next. My exhaustion was so extreme I could not fully comprehend my situation. When the guards arrived they had to pry my stiff fingers off the chain they had clutched for so long. A soldier motioned at me to get off the car:

'Come on, come on, get off, we don't have all day.'

I stared at him, or through him, thinking that I understood what he wanted me to do, but realizing that I could not do what he asked and not knowing how to tell him. I had lost all feeling in my legs. I looked down, willing them to move, but they just hung there. They felt to me like the limbs of the dead I had had to toss off the train, cold and foreign. The soldier pressed me.

'Dammit, are you deaf? Jump off already!' he spat, or something like it, in his American drawl.

He was clearly irritated and wanted to be done with this unpleasant business, and I was holding everything up.

I wanted nothing more than to get off. Willing myself to make a forward motion I fell off the car, hitting the ground face first, unable to brace myself with my numb arms and paralyzed from the waist down. I felt gritty dirt in my mouth and moved my face a little to the side so I could breathe. That was the end of the line for me. I could make it no further. I closed my eyes.

Eventually, somebody picked me off the ground and carried me to a truck, into which I was thrown like a sack of potatoes. There were probably more people than just me on that truck, but I wasn't fully conscious. I was dropped off at a *Lazarett*, a British military hospital. The British, who were the occupying force in the region, took over my care, and I stayed there for several weeks. When they took off my combat boots they found that my socks had fused themselves to my skin; as they took off my socks, the skin on my legs and feet went with them. They had to peel off the upper layer of my skin along with the fabric of the socks in long strips. The burning sensation was almost unbearable.

'You are lucky. This isn't hurting more because you still have so much numbness in your legs,' the nurse told me, while she was dabbing ointment on the raw flesh of my legs and feet and wrapping them in gauze bandages.

I appreciated what she was trying to do, but I did not feel so lucky.

As I got the feeling back in my feet, they tingled unbearably, as if an army of ants had burrowed inside them. The pain was intense. The nurses would change the dressings two or three times a day. My heavily bandaged legs had to be suspended by pulleys off the bed in mid-air, as they could not be in contact with any surface until the skin grew back, just like those of a burns victim. I would lie there all day, slipping in and out of a groggy sleep. Sometimes I dreamed I had finally been reunited with my mum and dad. In the dream it was always a warm, sunny day. They were both standing at the front door of our house, excitedly waving and smiling as I ran toward them with my arms open wide. And then I would wake up, and terror would grip my throat. *What if they're not there any more?*

Every day, the nurses would rub with alcohol the parts of my legs that were not raw and move them to force circulation. The feeling gradually started returning, although I was told that my nerves had been damaged and I might never regain full feeling in my legs. The

Brits fed me well. At five feet eleven inches tall, I weighed about 90lbs when I was admitted to the hospital, so they had to be careful because my stomach had shrunk so much it couldn't accept food. At first, they only fed me some kind of milk soup. This was made with real milk. Other than so-called skimmed milk, actually just thinned down with water, I had not seen milk in a couple of years. Only gradually did they start feeding me solid food.

I got to eat English food for the first time in my life. They had this bread or cake which they put in warm water, and the dough rose as it made contact with the liquid. It fascinated me and it was really tasty, so I kept asking the nurses for more, and they occasionally slipped me an extra portion.

The British treated us Germans as people. In their eyes I was a human being. I was grateful to them for that.

I had to relearn how to walk. The feeling never did fully return everywhere in my legs. From that time on I never felt my left foot again, except for the heel and part of the sole. The big toes on both feet were permanently warped, and the nails were dead. These injuries, along with the angry red bayonet scar running the length of my left calf, would stay with me as visible reminders of the war for the rest of my life. The other injuries I carried could not be seen as easily.

American policy in Germany

On 10 May 1945 President Truman approved JCS (Joint Chiefs of Staff) policy 1067, which instructed the US occupying forces in Germany to 'take no steps looking toward the economic rehabilitation of Germany, [nor steps] designed to maintain or strengthen the German economy.'

Food was scarce, and the German population went hungry. The food situation became critical during the bitterly cold winter of 1946/7, when German calorie intake sank to starvation levels, a situation made worse by the severe lack of heating fuel.

German heavy industry had been reduced to 50 per cent of its 1938 levels by the dismantling of around 1,500 factories. The problems brought on by these policies soon became obvious to US officials. Germany had long been the industrial powerhouse of Europe, and its lack of reconstruction was holding back the entire European recovery. The continued shortages in the country also led to considerable expense for the occupying powers.

The West's worst fear by now was that poverty and hunger would drive the Germans to Communism. General Lucius Clay famously stated, 'There is no choice between being a communist on 1,500 calories a day and a believer in democracy on a thousand.' It became apparent by 1947 that a change of policy was required.

The Truman administration eventually realized that economic recovery in Europe could make no progress without the reconstruction of the German industrial base. In July 1947, President Truman rescinded the punitive JCS 1067 on 'national security grounds' and replaced it with JCS 1779, which stressed that '[a]n orderly, prosperous Europe requires the economic contributions of a stable and productive Germany.'

Part IV

The Aftermath

Chapter 23

The Reunion

My wounds eventually healed, and I was discharged from the military hospital towards the end of July 1945, about one month after I had been released from the internment camp. The Tommies shoved a ticket in my hand and said I could go to Witten on a train free of charge. I was preoccupied with getting home as soon as possible, and finding my parents became my only priority. I rushed to the station and got on the very next train. Apprehension choked me every time I thought about what I would find. *What if they're dead? What will I do?*

I forced myself just to concentrate on getting there and stopped the reel in my mind from running any further.

Since the tracks were destroyed everywhere, this train also had to make a long detour, so that a trip that should have taken a little over an hour lasted the entire day. Along the way, a girl got on the train and sat down in my compartment. She was perhaps one or two years older than me. We said hello, and I asked her where she was going. She was going to Witten as well and was from the Witten-Annen area, where my best friend Kalla lived. His family ran an electrical appliance store there. I told her about it, and she knew the store.

It was obvious that I was a soldier, since I was wearing a uniform, the only clothes I owned.

Still, she asked, 'So, where are you coming from?'

'I … from the front. I was injured and have just been released from the hospital. I'm on my way home now.'

'Oh.'

After a rather long pause she added, 'Is this the first time you are back since you left for the war?'

'Yes. How is everything in Witten?'

A shadow fell across her face. She hesitated, looking at her hands in her lap.

'Witten is a dead city.'

I stared at her, willing her in my mind to take back what she had just said.

And then, blurting out the words in a torrent of emotion, she told me, 'Witten has been destroyed.'

She paused for a moment, tears welling up in her eyes.

'Our first serious bombing happened in December 1944, and then nothing. We thought we had got lucky … we thought we had been spared the worst. We were doing so much better than the other towns, you know. Duisburg, Dortmund, Essen and Bochum, they had all been destroyed before by the air raids. But then, in the end we got bombed to the ground on 19 March. So many people died …'

She stopped, as if collecting her thoughts. Her words punched me in the stomach. This was what I had dreaded. I was trying to process what she had said, praying it wasn't as bad as it sounded.

Looking down at the ground, she continued, 'The air raid warning went off at about 3.30 in the morning. My parents and I scrambled to take cover in the city centre bunker, which was safer than our old cellar. We were running with so many others that we lost my father in the crowd. My mum was hysterical, screaming for him, but then she looked at me, grabbed my hand and we kept on running. The sirens started howling full alarm a few minutes later, just as we made it to the bunker. I sat huddled in the dark with my mum and a bunch of strangers for a while. And then it started. The noise was so frightening. The earth shook. We thought this was finally it, Armageddon.'

My heart tightened in my chest as I listened to her story.

'When we finally got out, Witten was engulfed in flames. We couldn't make our way home the way we had come because of the mountains of rubble everywhere. As we tried to find an alternative route, the firemen kept pushing us back, shouting at us that they couldn't control the fires. As we finally got closer to our house we saw our church and my school in ruins. The house was still standing, we were so relieved, but explosions kept going off in the distance. The sky was blood-red, people were yelling. We didn't know where my dad was. It was awful ...'

Her voice trailed off. She looked out of the window, choking back tears. I just stared at her.

A moment later, in another burst of emotion, she almost shouted, 'And that was really messed up, what happened, because not even a couple of months later the war was over. Witten is 80 per cent destroyed. And we heard Churchill did this on purpose, targeting civilians ...'

I was afraid of what I was going to find. *Is there any chance my parents made it?* What would I do without them? Where would I go? I felt cold and clammy.

'Your father?' I managed to ask in a thin voice

'Alive, thank God. And your parents – do you know?'

She looked straight at me, her eyes wide.

I just shook my head. 'I don't.'

We didn't talk much after that, each of us inside our own heads, looking out of the window as the train kept passing the skeletal remains of devastated town after devastated town, its monotonous rhythm rocking us relentlessly ever closer to our destination.

As the train pulled into Witten, I saw shards of glass everywhere, the station in a shambles, the roof partly caved in. People were stepping over or around the debris to get on with their business. Suddenly the memory of the last time I had seen this station overcame me. It was when I had escaped from Konstanz to see my parents at Christmas 1943, so incredibly long ago. I was a child then, a little kid. It seemed like a distant memory of another life. And now, who was I? Definitely not that child anymore. I felt a pang of longing for a time long gone.

I didn't really want to know, but I had no choice. I made my way reluctantly out of the station, and then I saw it. Everything was flattened. I blinked, because the landscape was so unfamiliar that for a moment I could not get my bearings. Then I walked up the Bahnhofstrasse away from the station in the direction of the marketplace, and all I saw still standing was City Hall and some of the Protestant churches, although they were severely damaged. Then I looked toward the Catholic Church of Mary and the adjacent Marienhospital, and they still stood, although the hospital had suffered significant damage. The roof had caved in, the walls had gaping holes. My steps became heavier as I went on towards my street, the Johannisstrasse.

I steeled myself for what was to come. As I turned the corner, all my worst fears were realized. I stared in terror as I saw that what had been our house was completely destroyed; there was just a heap of rubble where it had once stood, a stake with a cardboard sign showing the street number planted in the middle of it.

I thought I might have been prepared for this because of what the girl on the train had told me, but that was just wishful thinking. The sight knocked the breath out of me. I sank to my knees, as much out of weakness as out of sorrow. I blinked hard a few times and swallowed as my fingers touched the rubble of my childhood. At that moment I was completely alone. I cried. Tears for my parents, for my dead friends, for all who suffered, for all that was lost.

I sensed panic fluttering just at the edge of my consciousness and made a herculean effort to stay focused. If I went to that dark place I somehow knew I wouldn't be able to come back. I made a decision. Mama and Papa are alive. I would find my parents, and everything would be all right. One thing I knew for sure, my father would have gone to Tante Mimi's at the Herbergerstrasse, because that was where the family always gathered when something was happening; so I decided to go there right away, praying it hadn't been bombed. I started decisively down the street and increased my pace as I got closer, the need to know suddenly urgent. I turned the corner.

I was right; no bombs had fallen there. The Herbergerstrasse was a funny street; as you approached it, there was a wall on the pavement, and you had to walk around it to continue on into the street. I stepped around the wall, and as I cleared it and looked up, there on the other side was my father. He looked as I remembered him, but I spied a bend in his spine and a frailness about him where there had been a stiff military bearing before. He seemed thinner. Relief mixed with apprehension overcame me. So much had happened since I had last seen him. My stomach tightened, and my heart pounded.

My pace quickened as I walked over to him. The distance to the house was about 30 or 40 metres. I was in full uniform, the uniform of the German Afrika Korps. The Americans had, of course, taken off all the insignia. The German eagle with the swastika and the shoulder lapels had all been torn off, leaving threads and gashes in the fabric. My father looked up briefly and must have just seen some soldier walking. I was wearing the soft fabric cap of Rommel's army, not a steel helmet. But then he looked up again, studied me and froze. I had imagined this moment so many times – my parents and I racing toward each other, falling into each other's arms, laughing and crying together. But he did not react like that at all. My throat tightened.

I walked up to him and tentatively said, 'Hallo, Papa.'

He looked at me and, without saying a word, turned on his heel and took off.

'But, Papa …?' I whispered, watching him walk away.

I did not run after him. The cold and crushing weight of despair bore down on me and took my breath away. I had lost him.

I stood there, stunned, for a long while, not knowing what to do with myself. Eventually, I decided to go to Tante Mimi and Onkel Hermann's house. I knocked, and Tante Mimi opened the door. A petite woman, her dark brown hair tidily arranged in a low bun, her left hand resting on her white lace-edged apron, she smiled politely at me for a second, thinking I was just another soldier, but then recognition set in.

She threw her arms around me and yelled, 'Hermann, Oma, you won't believe this! Our Willi is here! He's back, he's here, come quick!'

Onkel Hermann came hurrying down the long hallway, as fast as his stout frame permitted.

'Willi, *mein Gott*, Willi, it is so good to see you.'

He gave me a bit of a stiff hug and then shook my hand vigorously, grinning broadly. Oma was calling from the room.

'Where is Willi?'

'Let's go and see Oma,' said Onkel Hermann and rushed me into the dining room, where she was sitting with her knitting on her lap.

Although she had difficulty getting up she insisted on heaving herself out of her chair, impatiently waving off Onkel's offers of help.

'Oh, do stop fussing over me,' she grumbled while trying to gain her balance.

Once upright, she opened her arms and beckoned me over to give me a big hug.

'My, how much you have grown. You are a young man now.'

She patted my check, looking up at me, and smiled.

'You must be hungry. Get the boy some food, Mimi, he's just skin and bones. What happened to you, boy?'

'Oh, Oma, you know, the war and all …' My voice trailed off as I tried to think of what to say.

I turned to my aunt. 'Tante Mimi, Papa was outside and saw me, but he didn't talk to me and he just walked off.'

'Oh, Willi, don't worry, he's been preoccupied, you know, what with your house getting bombed and all. He'll be back soon, you'll see,' she said in a reassuring tone and went off to fetch some food from the kitchen.

'And Mama?' I asked as she walked away, fearful what the answer would be.

'Oh, she's fine, your Papa sent her to the farm to be safe,' she replied from the kitchen, raising her voice so I could hear.

I breathed a sigh of relief, nodded to myself and sat down with my Oma and Onkel Hermann, who peppered me with questions. It was a welcome distraction that kept me from slipping into the dark place in my mind that had no answer as to why my father had rejected me. It worked, at least for the time being.

While I left out most of the details, I told them that I'd been drafted into battle, taken prisoner by the Americans, then released and nursed back to health by the Tommies, who had given me a train ticket to get home. They stared at me in wide-eyed silence. I sensed they were uncomfortable by the glances they shot at each other, but they listened quietly to my story. At one point, when I looked straight at them, they averted their eyes. I wondered briefly why they were doing that but was too preoccupied with my father's reaction and my mother's absence to dwell on it.

'Well then, Willi, have some of this proper food here.'

Tante Mimi set a plate of steaming ham hocks with boiled potatoes and a helping of mustard in front of me. Famished, I wolfed the food down, barely even tasting it. The conversation quickly passed to them telling me how everybody was doing at home and away from the subject of my experiences.

Papa didn't come back, not that night or the next, or on any of the days I stayed in Witten. It tortured me not to know what I had done to him to make him so angry, but I could not reach him to find out.

During those days, Tante Mimi, Papa's sister, told me a lot of things I did not know. She reminded me that Papa had fought in the

First World War. He had lost friends and been severely wounded in the trenches, narrowly escaping with his life, only to have to relive the nightmare as a civilian in this second war. He saw his house with all his worldly belongings destroyed by a fire-bomb; it had set off a firestorm that could not be extinguished until it had consumed everything.

'Your Papa threw himself into the smouldering ruins,' Tante Mimi told me, 'to get to the cellar to save his medals from the First World War and his gun, and all the other things he held dear. The neighbours had to pull him off the burning rubble.'

In my mind's eye I saw Papa digging through the pile of debris our house had been reduced to, desperate to save a slice of his past, a piece of his identity to hold on to. Sadness filled my heart. A greater calamity could not have befallen him than to have his house taken from him, representing all that he had worked for in his life, and of which he was so proud.

My aunt also told me that one day in May 1945 a train had arrived with the children from Schleching.

'Your Papa rushed to the station and eagerly waited for his Willi to step off the train, but you never did. Then he asked the others, but they said, "We don't know where Willi is." His only child was missing; he feared you were dead.'

I listened in silence, thinking back to my father on the platform. I remembered how, when they first sent me away to Konstanz, he had kept pace with the departing train, waving goodbye to me until I disappeared in the distance.

'That was too much for your Papa. He could not bear to lose you. Shortly after that he suffered a heart attack.'

I felt sorry for Papa, sorry that I caused him so much suffering without knowing. Thinking about it later, I realized that fear had turned into anger, and my father's fear of having lost his only son had turned into uncontrollable rage at me for having put myself in harm's way. As if I'd had a choice. But I didn't blame him.

I was never able to tell my father where I had been. He never wanted to know. Although slowly, over time, we re-established our relationship, we never spoke of it. The pain was buried deep under the ruins of our houses, under the bodies of our dead, under the shame of total defeat and the obliteration of our identities.

We were the damned generation.

Chapter 24

Expectation Meets Reality

Within a few days of arriving in Witten I had to report to City Hall with my discharge papers from the American internment camp; this, incidentally, was the only proof of my existence, as all our family records had been destroyed in the bombing. There was a man at the counter who was known by the townspeople to be a communist and who had suffered imprisonment during the war at the hands of the Nazis. Emboldened by his newfound power, having been installed in this position of authority by the Allies, he berated me because I had been a soldier and he assumed I was a Nazi.

'Another one of you shit Nazis coming for handouts?'

'Oh, just kiss my arse,' I told him.

What else could he do to me that I hadn't gone through already? It was not as if he intimidated me, and it didn't matter any way. Nothing much mattered any more. The war had destroyed everything. I had witnessed and done terrible things, I had almost died at least twice, everything I knew was gone, my father did not want to see me, I had no future. I stared right back at him. He looked down at the papers. After he had punctiliously read the document from top to bottom with the clear intention of irritating me but seeing no way to delay any longer, he reluctantly stamped a document approving farm labour, and handed it to me along with my discharge papers and a couple of ration stamps for potatoes. Since it was written on my discharge papers that I was a student and farmer, he had to send me to work on a farm.

Expectation Meets Reality 143

As he handed me the documents he looked at me, the corners of his mouth turned down in disdain.

'Since you put down that you are a farmer, which I doubt, you have to go work on a farm for one year. You have eight days to figure it out, then you have to report to me where you will go and take off there.'

'Fine.'

I grabbed my papers and stormed out.

No sooner said than done. I went back to Tante Mimi's and told her I had been ordered to go work on a farm for one year, and that I had to leave town within one week. All my mother's brothers were farmers, and I guessed it shouldn't be difficult to find one who would take me. My mum's was a large, close-knit family. Tante Mimi recommended I should go to my Onkel Franz's farm in Brenken to complete this year of forced labour. Since Onkel Franz was the eldest son and had inherited the family farm, he ran the biggest and most profitable outfit with the most work, so I would be well taken care of there.

Tante Mimi is right. It won't be so bad, it's Onkel Franz after all. I believed that although I was going to be forced to work on a farm for a period of a year and could not leave, the fact that I was going to a relative would make it bearable, despite the delay in my going back to school and resuming some kind of normal life. It seemed to be one more thing that just had to be got over and done with.

The only nagging issue was that I couldn't talk to either of my parents about this decision. My father was avoiding me. Since our encounter the day I arrived, he had not been back to the house, and we didn't know where he had gone. As for my mother, she had not been back since my father had sent her to her family in Brenken in March, and Tante Mimi didn't know exactly who she was staying with. Given that nobody had a telephone, and the post was slow, there was no good way of finding out other than going to Brenken and finding her. I ached for my mother, for her loving and protecting arms. I knew I would be able to tell her everything, and she would listen, she would understand my pain.

The eighth day came soon enough. Not wanting to run foul of the authorities, I made sure to report in at City Hall and leave on that day. I didn't have much to take with me on my trip. In a small suitcase Tante Mimi packed a few sausage sandwiches for me, one pair of underpants and a waistcoat I got as a hand-me-down from my cousins. I still wore my frayed uniform, the only clothing I owned.

I made my way to the station. There were no direct connections to where I was going. One had to take a train to the town of Paderborn, and then a connecting train from there to Brenken.

The disruption caused by the bombing of the track was so severe that the few trains in operation were overcrowded, and when I got to the platform I found there was no space on the train. There were people pressed up against doors of the carriages and spilling over to the outside. However, there was a step and a vertical handle on the outside of each door, and I was so determined to leave that I decided to stand on the step and hold on to the handle. And so, holding on with my left hand and grasping the suitcase in my right, I dangled there half inside and half outside of the train as it took off, then held on for dear life as we travelled on for hours.

The wind kept whipping me, particularly if I moved, so hard that it weakened my footing and threatened to rip the suitcase from my hand. I tried to stand still and press my body flush against the carriage door. The noise of the wind and the clanking of the metal wheels on the tracks was deafening, and the wind hit my face so hard that it became numb. A couple of times my feet slipped a little, and I struggled desperately to inch them back on to their precarious perch, afraid to look down or to make any move that might make me lose my balance and throw me off the train. As we finally made our first stop in the city of Zost, shortly before reaching Paderborn, I thought I was going to fall off. I was completely stiff. I could not move and my fingers were stuck in place, curled around the handle.

My mind flashed back to the cattle train that took us home, when my legs were so numb they stopped working and I almost died. I felt a wave of nausea and dizziness overtake me and I stumbled, losing my footing. Luckily, some people noticed me; I think they saw my uniform and decided to help.

'Hey, boy, hold on, we'll get you inside,' I heard a man say.

I felt arms grabbing me and pulling me and somehow managing to haul me inside the train. I landed on someone and mumbled, 'So sorry, thank you' at nobody in particular. Friendly faces greeted me, and people patted my back.

'It's OK, *Junge*, it's OK,' I heard, and I smiled, trying not to bump into too many people as the train chugged along. People were being helpful and nice to me and I appreciated it, but it made me feel awkward. I didn't know what to say, other than muttering *'Danke'* a few times. I wasn't used to kindness any more.

I got off in Paderborn and boarded the train to Brenken. Moving closer towards the place that was to become my compulsory home for the next year, I decided that, despite putting my life on hold, the experience would not be too tough. How could it possibly be? They were my family, after all.

* * *

I was the only one to get off the train in Brenken. I walked along the tracks for about fifty metres before arriving at a level crossing that was protected with a barrier; it was up since no more trains were coming that summer afternoon. After a short while the first house of the town of Brenken came into view where my uncle Heinrich Hardes lived. He was the twelfth and youngest of my mother's siblings.

I paused just before reaching the bend in the road that led to his house, some force preventing me from continuing on my way. My legs had become heavy and sluggish. I felt a sudden urge to walk up to Onkel Heinrich's house, knock at his door and ask him to take me in, instead of going to Onkel Franz's. I stopped in the middle of the street as thoughts flooded my mind. Onkel Heinrich was my favourite uncle and a very smart man. He had been an inspiration to me. With the little money he had received from his inheritance when my grandparents passed away, together with a little he had borrowed, he had built himself this farm. He bought for a pittance land that nobody wanted. It was poor land, and everybody mocked him, thinking he was stupid. But Onkel Heinrich had an especially keen eye for modern inventions. Artificial fertilizer had been introduced during Nazi times, and he purchased a lot of it and spread it on the land. Either the man had an incredible stroke of good luck or was just very clever, but this land that nobody wanted and that he had bought for next to nothing started yielding like mad. I always thought that was really something. Maybe I could stay with him, and he could teach me a few things.

A fly buzzed by my ear, and I realized I was standing in the middle of the street daydreaming. Reluctantly, I walked on.

On most days when the train arrived in Brenken one would find Onkel Heinrich's wife Gertrud, a jolly, chubby woman with permanently red cheeks, standing at the front door of the house to greet those who had got off the train. Sure enough, she walked out of the front door just as I was standing there around the bend with my little suitcase. She recognized me immediately and shouted out to me, waving her hand high over her head.

'Willi! Hello, how is you, my boy?' she greeted me in typical Brenken fashion.

I shouted back, 'Hello, Tante Gertrud. Considering the circumstances, not so great. I was at the front, our house was bombed, and I can't find my parents. I have been ordered by the authorities to work on the land, so I am going to Onkel Franz's to work at his farm.'

Onkel Franz lived just a few houses further down the road. As I started walking towards it, Tante Gertrud responded.

'Oh, I see. Well, well, Willi, you have to come to our house soon and get something to eat. I'll bake you a nice cake.'

'Thank you Tante Gertrud, I will do that.'

I waved and continued on my way.

The village main street ran past the station, and Onkel Heinrich's was the first house on the right. The street then curved to the left, and Onkel Franz's house, my grandfather's ancestral farm, was on the left just past the bend. It was built in the traditional way, a large farmhouse with whitewashed walls and dark wooden crossbeams along the front and sides of the building, windows with wooden shutters and colourful window boxes. The long street continued over a bridge under which ran a small river called the Alme. Despite its size it was a very treacherous stream, with undercurrents that could sweep a grown man away and pull him under. It had caused many a tragic accident. The river's waters ran dark. A cloud obscured the sun for a moment, and a shiver ran up my spine. I shook off the uneasy feeling, composing myself.

I finally arrived at Onkel Franz's farm and knocked on the door. Anxiety suddenly gripped me. What would I find on the other side? It had been a long time since I had seen anybody there, and nobody knew I was coming.

I heard footsteps approaching.

The door opened, and there stood my mother. Although I had known that she was in the countryside staying with family, I didn't know that she was at Onkel Franz's. I had meant to ask Onkel Franz where I could find her.

I saw her eyes widen in surprise. My heart skipped a beat. She threw her arms around me:

'Our Willi! Oh, my God, Jesus, Mary and Joseph, our Willi, where did you spring from?'

'Mama!' I sobbed.

I was so happy I felt I could not breathe. I fell into her arms and squeezed my eyes shut, holding her tight, believing for just that one moment that the universe was all right again. *Everything is going to be OK now.*

The words poured out of me: 'I come from the war, Mama. I was fighting at the front. I was taken prisoner.'

The floodgates had opened, and I cried out to her, 'I saw Papa, but I could not tell him anything, he didn't want to hear anything!'

She looked at me with a startled sadness in her eyes and said firmly, 'Oh, Willi, hush, don't talk nonsense about being in the war. You were perhaps with the anti-aircraft gun patrol, not really in the war. You're confused.'

'No, Mama, it's true!' I pleaded with her.

'Oh, son, hush already, don't tell me any more war stories. Let me look at you, my boy. You are home.'

She wasn't having it.

'But I was …'

Then I stopped. I looked at her and saw in her eyes the sheer joy at having her boy back, but also, tucked away in the back, a glimmer of fear, perhaps of things she did not want to hear. I decided to keep my mouth shut. How could I ruin the happiness of the only person who genuinely and unconditionally loved me, whom I had so yearned to be with again? Selfishly, I craved that love, even at the cost of having to stay silent.

Along came my aunt Theresa, running into the vestibule and giving me a big, crushing hug, enveloping me in her large embrace. Onkel Franz, every bit as robust and red-cheeked as she was, walked in behind her. As it was just after lunchtime he was still home from the fields. And behind him came their children, my first cousins. Onkel Franz and Tante Theresa had three sons, Hannes, Heini and Franz. They also had two daughters, Maria and Anna. Maria, or Mia as we called her, was a year older than me, sixteen, and the one to whom I had always been closest. The boys were between eight and seventeen years old, so luckily they had been spared the war by virtue of living in a rural area. The parents had pulled Franz, the eldest, from school under the pretext of needing him to work full-time in the fields, and this had secured him exemption from compulsory military service.

Anna was the baby at only seven. She was nicknamed *Kohlenklau*, coal thief, after a wartime cartoon character representing a person who wasted energy. Posters of him were put up everywhere, and there was a popular *Kohlenklau* board game we loved to play. You would roll the dice and if you landed on *Kohlenklau* doing something that wasted energy like 'leaving the radio on when nobody is listening' you had to sit out a turn. The character's face was covered in soot, and he carried a sack of coal on his back. Anna was a very messy eater and would smear whatever she ate over her face, which made her look like the soot-covered cartoon character and always made us laugh.

They all hugged me, including messy Anna, who held on to my trouser leg and promptly rubbed her grubby face into it, leaving a big stain. Onkel Franz shook my hand vigorously.

'My good boy, so good to have you back. Your mother was distraught. The poor woman didn't know what to do with herself.'

After a lot of backslapping and rejoicing, we sat down at the dining room table.

'Theresa, bring out some coffee and pastries for everybody. This is a special occasion,' bellowed Onkel Franz as he settled his huge frame in a chair that groaned under his weight.

This is when I told Onkel Franz and my mother about the discharge paper conditions that obliged me to undertake one year of forced farm labour, and how Tante Mimi had suggested I go to him.

'I see,' he said, inspecting the paper and scratching his chin pensively. His demeanour shifted perceptibly from jovial to circumspect.

'Just a minute. I'll be right back.'

He went into the kitchen, and I heard him talking to Tante Theresa in hushed tones. One of the boys also went into the kitchen and then out of the back door on the other side of it. When my aunt and uncle came back into the dining room, I sensed something had changed. They were smiling a bit stiffly, sitting very straight in their chairs. Tante Theresa was fidgeting with her napkin. My mother didn't seem to be concerned, however, and was chatting about this and that, so happy that I was there that nothing else seemed to matter.

'Bless the Lord, my boy is back. My boy! We have to tell everybody. We are going to see Heinrich and Gertrud, and Franz Bach and Johanna …' and on she went, holding my hand and squeezing it and patting it. She couldn't take her eyes off me. 'My boy, you are so thin. Theresa, put a little more cake on his plate my dear, you can see he's starving.'

I felt happy but overwhelmed. I had dreamed of my return for so long, how joyful my reunion with both of my parents would be, but then it had gone so terribly wrong with my father, for reasons I still could not fully grasp, that I was almost scared to let myself be too happy in case I was knocked back again. So I sat there dazed, feeling distant, although I didn't want to. Things had changed, I had changed and I felt that I no longer fitted in the way I had before everything happened. The war had put a distance between us that I didn't know if I could bridge.

We stayed at the table for a long while. More relatives came and went as the word of my return spread. Dinner was served, and afterwards people went back to their homes. My mother reluctantly told me that she had a very important appointment the next day in Witten which she could not miss with a city official about obtaining a permit to rebuild our home. She was going to have to leave first thing in the morning but was going to try to come back as soon as possible. I could see she was very unhappy about having to leave me.

'You will take good care of my boy, Franz, you hear?' she said.

'Yes, about that, Maria, come here, I need a quick word …' Onkel Franz replied and took her aside.

Just at that moment, my aunt Theresa asked me if I wanted more food and I became distracted, so that I didn't hear what he said to her.

The emotions of the day had drained me, my awareness was slipping, but I noticed my mother did not seem happy. Something was bothering her, she was frowning.

My uncle suddenly announced loudly, 'Come on, son, let's get you settled. We'll show you to your room. It's high time we all went to bed because we have to get up early, and your mother has a train to catch, don't you, Maria?'

My mother was still frowning but she came up to me and gave me a big, long hug.

'I love you, son. I will be back soon.'

She let go reluctantly.

'Follow me,' boomed uncle Franz.

I turned around to see my mother standing hesitantly in the middle of the living room.

'Bye, Mama,' I waved.

'Bye, son …' she waved back, a little weakly.

Then I followed Onkel Franz. We went outside through the back door, the same door my cousin had used earlier when he went into the kitchen to talk to his parents. I found this a bit odd, because it meant we were leaving the main farmhouse and heading to the adjacent buildings which were mostly stables. When we got to the room, which was not in the main building, it wasn't much to look at; only a bed with a straw-filled mattress, whitewashed walls, a stone floor and a damp smell permeating it. Then I sensed a presence and saw another person standing there in a corner. He was the farm hand Fritz Freudewald, who I soon learned had been a sailor in the war. I suspected, correctly, that he was also staying in this room. *OK, bunking with the farm hand? Maybe there isn't any room elsewhere.*

'Hello there. Fritz is the name. And yours?' he stuck out his hand decisively, a broad grin on his face.

'Hello. I am Willi.'

I shook his hand. He seemed friendly enough.

I was put on stable duty. I had to get up at five in the morning, and my first task was to clean out the cow barn, then the pigsty. The animals had to be seen to first, and after that the humans could take a turn at having breakfast. Onkel Franz and Tante Theresa sat at the head of the table, surrounded by their children. I was seated at the very end of the table with the farmhand Fritz. Our breakfast consisted of a malt beverage made from roasted wheat with water poured over it and a little sugar added. Fritz and I got a slice of bread with beet butter spread on it rather sparingly, while the others had a fat sandwich, with butter spread an inch thick and fried eggs to go with it.

Are you joking? I only weighed about 90lbs when I was released from the internment camp, and I weighed just over 110lbs when I left the British hospital. At five feet eleven I was literally just skin and bones, and I was still growing. How ironic to finally be settled with my family and, instead of celebrating my safe return, to find myself moving in with the farmhand Fritz Freudewald and being fed little more than the starvation rations I got at the internment camp, when there was an obvious abundance of food around. I thought back to the time when I was four years old, when we took Opa's and Oma's golden anniversary picture at Onkel Franz's farm and Tante Bernhardine piled the food high on my plate. *Am I not the same nephew? What happened to them?* I did complain to my mother when I saw her again, which turned out to be quite a while later, and she confronted her brother about it, but he told her, 'Willi has been ordered to come here. He is obliged to work after all, so he is going to be treated just like our stable boy.'

It seemed that my uncle Franz had been pleased to have this opportunity fall in his lap, and he wasn't going to waste it. Free labour, after all, was hard to pass up, so what did it matter if it was a relative? Particularly one who couldn't leave.

What a joy this family was turning out to be, I concluded with the cynicism I had started to develop. But I determined I was going to get over it, just as I had overcome so many of the other things I had experienced. Nobody had yet managed to bring me to my knees.

Chapter 25

Onkel Franz's Farm

Life at the farm was predictably tough and monotonous. At five in the morning I cleaned the pigsty, and Fritz milked the cows, then we had breakfast and went back to work. At around nine we got a so-called second breakfast, which was as frugal as the first, and after that we rode out with the horses to the fields and worked there the rest of the day. I learned how to manage a double-furrow plough, the *doppel Schar Pflug*. The plough's steel blades were dragged through the soil by two heavy draught horses, turning over the upper layer of earth and creating deep furrows for the next planting. It was a tricky job, as I had to steady and manoeuvre the plough to ensure it moved in a straight line and didn't get stuck on big stones, steering it by holding on to its V-shaped handles and walking over the loose ploughed soil, all the while holding the horses' reins so they would not walk out of line while I was handling the plough.

I was often working in a field that was about five to seven kilometres away from the farm, completely by myself. My cousin Mia would ride out to the field on her bike at lunchtime and bring me a canteen, like in the military, with potatoes, vegetables and some meat. I also got a bottle of thin malt coffee with a little sugar. It wasn't much, but it was better than nothing. I seldom saw milk and butter. Mia was typically the only person I would interact with all day.

'Hey, Willi!' she would yell to get my attention as she rode up on her big white bike along a narrow path flanked by tall grass that marked the boundary between fields, a basket with my lunch hanging from the handlebar. I was always happy to see her and to take a break. I would hold a hand up high and wave to let her know I had heard or seen her coming.

'Here is your stuff,' she would say cheerfully as she spread a small cloth on the ground, placing the canteen and the jug on it, impatiently pushing aside her long blonde braids that always got in the way when she bent over.

She would usually stay for a few minutes and give me some gossip about local farmers, and when I had finished eating, she'd grab the implements and ride off again. Mia cared. That always made me feel a little better, a little less numb.

At around six I would harness the horses and haul the plough on to the wagon so it would not get stolen. I would then get on one of the horses and ride slowly back to the farm, usually arriving around seven. First, I had to unsaddle and take the harness off the horses and put everything away in the stables. After that there was a rather meagre dinner at the farmhands' end of the family table, before retiring for the night.

Given the circumstances, I felt friendlier toward Fritz Freudenwald than toward my blood relatives, and we got along famously. I would often take off with him on Sundays. Fritz had a girlfriend in the village. He was popular with the girls, but I was no big hit with the ladies, just not the type. I had bright red hair and lots of freckles. In the Third Reich there was a saying that went: *Rotes Haar und Sommersprossen machen die besten Volksgenossen*, red hair and freckles make the best patriots. I think they said that to console us gingers for not being as popular with the ladies as those with fair or dark hair. I didn't really mind, because I didn't know how to behave around girls anyway.

One Sunday afternoon I accompanied Fritz to see his girlfriend, and I was invited inside with him. Fritz's girlfriend's father was a manual worker. I knew from my mother that there was some tension in the village. The farmers thought themselves superior to the workers, and they never married into the working class. It had something to do with the fact that they owned land, and they were proud to the point of arrogance. They maintained that the workers were brutish and uneducated, as if the farmers themselves had much education. I thought this was silly and had no problem at all mixing with Fritz or his girlfriend. As we arrived at his girlfriend's house, Fritz casually mentioned she had a twin sister, whom Fritz had not told me about before, perhaps intending to set me up with her. We were shown into the living room and sat on the good couch with flowery upholstery and doilies on the armrests, the parents sitting across from us in matching armchairs. There was a plate of biscuits on the coffee table which everybody was too awkward to touch. I sat down next to the twin sister. I did not know what to do with myself, sitting stiffly straight and holding very still so as not to touch her or anything else if I could help it.

Suddenly, out of nowhere, my mother stormed into the room like a fury.

'Willi, get out right now, you are much too young, get out of here! You cannot sit here with girls and a sailor, that is not happening!'

I almost jumped out of my skin. My face and ears were burning, probably glowing redder than my hair. I just wanted to disappear.

'Let's go now, Willi,' my mother said in a steely voice, staring me down.

Utterly mortified, I silently followed my mother as she strutted out of the house, her head held very high. I was staring at the ground in front of me, feeling everybody's eyes burning a hole in the back of my head.

It turned out my mother had come from Witten that day, and my cousin Hannes had told on me.

'Tante Maria, go to so and so's house in Brenken. Fritz Freudewald the stable boy has gone there with Willi. He has a girlfriend who has a twin sister, and maybe Willi is sitting there with her.'

It definitely bothered my mother that I should get mixed up with girls, devout Catholic that she was. But it somehow bothered my mother even more that my best friend was a stable boy who worked at my uncle's farm. She was caught up in class snobbery like the rest of them. But Fritz wasn't just my co-worker, he was my friend. We laughed a lot, and we got one over on the farmers every time we could. In 1945 the summer was very rainy. Onkel Franz had grown wheat, and when it was harvested, we had to make sheaves, each of them bound with twine. We stood the sheaves against each other so they would not topple over, but because it was raining so much the ears of wheat began to sprout, and we were sent to the field on a Sunday with the task of breaking up the sheaves so that they would not grow into each other.

On our way there Fritz said, 'Willi, do you feel much like working?'

'No,' I said. 'No, I really don't.'

'You know what we're going to do? We're going to lie down, and we're going take a nap.'

I agreed enthusiastically and added, 'And when we get home we tell them we took the sheaves apart. By the time they show up here to check on it next week and complain that the sheaves are a mess, we'll tell them they must have grown back together since Sunday.'

We settled down for a nice nap. But who should happen to come past but this arsehole from the farm next door, owned by the Nazi family who had tried to get my grandfather Johannes in trouble before the war. He was the youngest brother of the lot. He saw us sleeping and promptly went to my uncle's and told on us. When I got home, Onkel Franz was waiting for me on the porch, arms crossed over his chest.

'Wilhelm, you are a relative of ours, Fritz is a *Prolet* [a manual worker]. He is employed as a farmhand, you cannot fraternize with this stable boy and do things with him.'

That was enough. I looked him straight in the eye.

'Well, Onkel Franz, then you should move me from the bottom of the table where I sit with Fritz and put me with you at the head of the table where there is more to eat.'

Onkel Franz looked at me in stunned disbelief.

'What? Go on, get out of here!'

He turned red in the face, balled his fists and hurried off to the barn.

He never moved me to the head of the table, but he never mentioned my fraternizing with the farmhand again.

Chapter 26

The Occupying Forces

The occupation was visible in the countryside, too. Allied troops patrolled all areas, making their presence known. Westphalia, with the towns of Witten and Brenken, was occupied by the British. What was to later become West Germany was divided into a British, a French and an American zone, and we Germans called this territory 'Trizonesia', on account of it being split into three. The part that became the DDR, East Germany, was under Russian control.

One weekend, Mama came to visit me at the farm. She had some interesting ideas about the British and the Dutch. One thing she was certain of was that she could communicate with them. Foreign languages were not a concept she fully grasped, and despite my best efforts to convince her that you actually had to learn someone else's language, she felt that if you just put in enough effort you would be able to talk to one another.

It was mid-morning on Sunday, my day off; the cows had been milked and the pigs tended to, and we were all sitting in the kitchen where Mama was helping my aunt to prepare breakfast. Suddenly three British soldiers burst through the front door, boisterous and loud, waving their guns and making themselves look important because they could.

'All right, everybody stand up. Let me see your hands. What is going on here?'

We stood up cautiously, holding our hands where they could see them, wary and mindful not to upset them.

One of them was a Sergeant, with three upward-pointing stripes, another was a Corporal, who had two, and the third was a Lance Corporal, who only had one. In that moment I noticed the random fact that this was different to the Americans I had encountered in the camp, whose stripes pointed downward. The Sergeant strutted through the kitchen towards my mother who, having first taken care to remove the eggs she was frying from the stove, was just turning around, wiping her hands on her apron.

Then Mama, who was not shy, started to talk to the Englishmen in *Brenkener Platt*, the Westphalian dialect. She had told herself, 'English must be like Brenkener Platt, so they have to understand me.' She looked the Englishman straight in the eye and asked, '*Willst en Paar Egger haem?*' which means, 'Do you want a couple of eggs?', and the Tommy understood '*Egger*'.

'Eggs, yes,' he said eagerly, his face lighting up in recognition and in joyful anticipation of a nice breakfast.

As the now friendly Tommies, all smiles, put their guns down on the big solid wood kitchen table and took a seat, ready to be fed, my mother turned to me.

'There, you see? They speak perfect *Brenkener Platt.*'

This incident cemented my mother's belief. She was henceforth convinced that all Englishmen understood *Brenkener Platt*.

* * *

While there were a few British soldiers around, the occupying forces in Brenken were mostly Yugoslavian. A lot of Yugoslavs had entered British service after the war, and they had received uniforms, but these were dark blue, not khaki like the British uniforms, so they were easily recognizable. These guys caused a lot of trouble in the village, stealing, fighting and molesting the girls. Eventually, the mayor of Brenken decided to set up a night watch, since a lot of the problems happened after dark. We did not have weapons but we did have our knives and pitchforks, with which you could stab somebody quite effectively if necessary. My uncle Heinrich and other men would stand watch every night. One man was stationed at one end of the village by the station, and another stood at the other end of the village. Whenever there was trouble they would blow a whistle, and all the farmers would jump out of bed and run to defend the villagers from looting or rape. There was nobody else to turn to; you had to take matters into your own hands.

Rumour had it that the miller, who worked by the bridge over the River Alme, and who always had a ladder leaning against the wall, would have his ladder occasionally borrowed by one or another of the night watchmen. The ladder was allegedly used to engage in '*fensterln*' as they said in Bavaria, which means window-courting. *Fensterln* was done with the *Mägde*, the farm maids. They were the female counterparts of the *Knechte*, the male farmhands. They were poor working-class girls from the village who took on this menial work to make ends meet, and they were rumoured to be prepared to receive friendly male visitors at midnight, perhaps for a small fee, or maybe just for fun or to escape their everyday routine. Everybody did what they had to do to survive. It was an open secret, and the men all joked about it.

Chapter 27

Sunday Mass

Time passed slowly at the farm. By now it was late autumn, and the days blended into each other with no end in sight and no meaning beyond the immediate needs of the animals that had to be fed and fields that required tending. It was a hard, numbing routine and in a way that was good; it helped to push out thoughts I did not want to have about things I did not want to remember. The war was a raw wound that was not healing. At the same time, I wanted to escape from this limbo I was in, neither home nor away, done with the war but still beholden to it. I had no idea what my future would hold, but I did know I wanted to be done with this. I wanted to be free.

'Willi, wake up, mate. It's OK, wake up.' Fritz was shaking my arm.

I had been screaming again. It was the nightmares. They sneaked up on me every night when my mind was unprotected.

'Sorry to wake you up …' I mumbled.

'It's OK, it's time to get up anyway.'

Fritz rummaged around for his clothes. It was Sunday, and time for church. We could not break our fast until we had been to church and taken holy communion. Luckily, mass was early in the morning.

The bells started pealing, calling the faithful. We walked out on to the main street toward the church, past the bend and over the bridge, and on the way more and more people joined us. As I was talking to Fritz, something caught my eye. A girl with raven-black hair was just stepping out on the street. I slowed my pace and turned my head to get a better look, and at that moment our eyes met. She had startlingly bright blue eyes. Embarrassed, I looked down and picked up my pace again. She was the most beautiful creature I had ever seen.

'What's up Willi? You OK?' asked Fritz.

'Yeah, mate. I just saw this girl …'

'Who, where?'

Fritz dug me in the ribs.

I gestured in her direction and mentioned the hair. Fritz picked her out and smiled.

'Nice. We're going to make sure we sit in the same pew.'

Fritz was already working on engineering a chance meeting so we could 'accidentally' get to talk to the girl. Sure enough, he managed to get us close and somehow introduce ourselves to her. She was easy to talk to, and we chatted all the way back to her house.

'Hey, Fritz, I'll catch up with you later,' I said.

I stopped at her front door with her, not really wanting to leave. She lingered by the door.

'So, where do you live?' she asked, and I pointed up the road and told her about Onkel Franz and how I really didn't live there, that I was on forced labour detail from the war, and where I was from, and many, many other things.

And she listened. And she laughed and told me things about herself. We stood there and chatted for at least an hour until her mother called her to go inside. I walked home as if floating on a cloud, my heart lighter than it had ever felt before.

Her name was Lotte. Her father was a manual worker, undesirable from my family's point of view. But that was the least of my worries. From that day on, every Sunday after church, we would stand in front of her house and talk. We talked and talked for hours about anything and everything, and those hours seemed like seconds when I was with her. I couldn't talk to anybody at the farm, but I could talk to her. She was a breath of fresh air in my life.

From that point on, every time Fritz had the opportunity he would tell whoever wanted to listen that I had a platonic love interest in

Brenken. It was true, our relationship was platonic; I never touched her or gave her a kiss. We just connected. Of course, my mother got wind of it and wasn't pleased. She would have preferred that I became acquainted with the daughter of the rich farmer by the church, who had three times more land than my uncle, but that girl did not like me, and the feeling was mutual. I wasn't interested in any of that matchmaking business anyway and didn't care whether my mother approved of my relationship or not. I just enjoyed finally having somebody I could talk to and share my thoughts and feelings with, somebody who didn't judge me or expect anything from me. She was somebody with whom, a few moments at a time, I could forget the shadow of war.

Chapter 28

The Bootlegging Incident

The farmers of Brenken were a crafty and enterprising lot and they had obtained from the blacksmith a still with which you could make schnapps out of wheat. They would put the still, a sort of high-pressure kettle, on a coal-fired stove, then the mixture in the kettle would heat up and the alcohol would be distilled out. This concoction was then put through a coal-filled filter to remove impurities. I tried it and, well, let me say you had to have a special palate to drink the stuff.

Obviously, this was bootlegging and strictly prohibited, but that didn't stop anybody. There was an alcohol tax, a very high one, and illegal distilling was a crime against the tax code which was severely punished. However, every last farmer would distil for his own consumption as well as to sell. The process would always be conducted at night so as not to draw any undue attention. You had to be careful, as the kettle would get extremely hot and could explode. There was a thermometer on it to monitor the temperature. When the thermometer reached the red mark, it was high time to remove the kettle from the fire or the whole thing would blow up.

Alcohol-laden vapours were released during the distilling process. One night, Onkel Heinrich, while brewing a batch, inhaled the vapours and dozed off into a semi-drunken sleep. Luckily, I was out and about that winter night and had decided to stop at Onkel Heinrich's. I thought he might be distilling some schnapps again, and maybe he'd let me try a sip or two of the brew which, although evil-tasting, would get you nicely warmed up.

'Hi, Onkel Heinrich, it's me,' I announced but got no reply.

The door was unlocked, so I walked in.

I immediately realized the danger. Onkel Heinrich was slumped over in his armchair fast asleep, a heavy smell of booze permeating the air. My eyes darted to the kettle. The thermometer was almost on red. I only had a few seconds. I ran over and pulled the kettle from the flame, burning my hands, then jumped to the chair and frantically shook my uncle awake.

'Onkel Heinrich, wake up, wake up, we have to run! Now!'

I knew I couldn't drag him out, he was a very big man, but I still tried to pull him from the chair. Finally, he started coming to and looked at me in a daze.

'Let's go, now!' I shouted.

Then he reacted. He realized what was going on and together we tumbled out of the door. In trying to help him out, we both tripped and fell on our arses just outside the front door. We sat in the cold moonlit street, listening intently for an explosion, but the kettle did not blow up.

After a few minutes Onkel Heinrich said, 'Thanks, son. Help me up, would you?'

Onkel Heinrich walked back in the house, put the kettle back on the stove and, cool as a cucumber, proceeded to continue distilling his schnapps.

I often wished I had been assigned to work at his farm instead of Onkel Franz's, but it would have never worked, because Onkel Franz was the patriarch and would have laid claim to me regardless. He would never have allowed his baby brother to take advantage of free farm labour before him. It was his birthright to take the first cut of everything. There was not much I could do but bide my time until this was over, and maybe one day things would be normal again. Although I wasn't sure I knew what normal meant any more.

Chapter 29

Mischief with Fritz Freudewald

After Mass one fine Sunday in the early spring of 1946, Onkel Franz harnessed two fresh horses to his carriage and left with Tante Theresa and their kids, clad in their Sunday best, in the direction of Lippe to spend the day with relatives who lived there. Fritz and I were left at the farm by ourselves.

Fritz looked at me and said, 'Willi, now let's have a little fun. We're going to make the pigs drunk.'

That sounded like a fantastic idea to me. For this special occasion we swiped two bottles of Onkel Franz's bootleg schnapps from the barn and poured it over the pigs' feed, having first taken a couple of swigs ourselves. If you know pigs, you know they will eat and drink anything and everything you put in front of them, which is exactly what they did. Then we opened their pens, and the pigs rushed outside to the *Misthaufen*, the dung pile, and ran around like the devil was on their tails, squealing and snorting all the time.

I had a great idea.

'Let's ride them, Fritz.'

Wasting no time, Fritz and I scrambled after the pigs and caught up with them in the slippery mess. We managed to jump on the backs of a couple of fat drunken sows and rode around on them, laughing so hard we could hardly hold on, slipping off and getting back on, completely covered in dung. Unfortunately, Onkel Franz and family suddenly appeared around the corner in their nice carriage and froze, staring in shocked disbelief at the spectacle in front of them. It turned out they were back from Lippe early because the relatives had not been at home. Needless to say, we had a little extra work given to us that day and were punished by going to bed without dinner. Given the small size of our usual lunch, the lack of dinner was painful, which was exactly what Onkel Franz had intended. Nonetheless, we had had a great laugh, and despite his best efforts, Onkel Franz could not take that away from us.

Chapter 30

The Fire Brigade

The anaemic size of the helpings and general stinginess about food at Onkel Franz's was symptomatic of a disease the farmers had caught during the war. It was called greed. Farmers are naturally a shrewd, some would say a cunning, lot, bred over generations to survive the harsh conditions of farming life, full of uncertainty and exposed to the whim of the elements. Bad weather or disease can devastate an entire year's crop almost overnight and leave a farmer penniless. Those that survived such insecurity had developed coping skills over time that involved the ability to ferret out any opportunity to make money.

Then suddenly, during the war, the Brenken farmers had come into more money than they could ever have dreamed of, because Adolf Hitler bought everything, every pound of wheat or meat they produced, for good money to feed German troops and German households. And predisposed as they were already to the love of money, once they acquired this wealth they fell prey completely to the disease of greed. They became determined to hold on to their money at any cost, which seemed to include shamelessly starving and exploiting family members, as well as devising clever plots to cheat the government, since from where they sat it appeared to have deep pockets.

A favourite scheme in town was insurance fraud. Surprisingly, several farmers in Brenken owned rather modern houses. The village had been in existence for centuries and one might have thought that they would have older dwellings, perhaps in poor shape, but that was not the case. The home insurance business had started in the twenties, and the farmers began insuring their homes, particularly against fire. Once insured, the town's farmhouses developed a tendency to burn down, especially during the annual *Schützenfest* festival, because at that time the volunteer fire brigade almost certainly wasn't able to make it out on time, as all the firemen were passed out drunk.

The town had a fire station equipped with an interesting fire-extinguishing apparatus, a cistern that had to be immersed in the River Alme to be filled up. Once full, the cistern was mounted on a wooden horse-drawn wagon and taken to the fire; a hand-operated pump then expelled a spray of water. Depending on how diligent and sober the firemen were, the spray would hit the mark and reach over the roof to douse the flames. If the water didn't reach, they would move progressively closer until they got within range.

At the time of the *Schützenfest* in May 1946, my Onkel Franz happened to be the captain of the volunteer fire brigade. Predictably, that evening, a shot went off signalling that there was a fire in Brenken. Onkel Franz, rather tipsy, set about gathering his troops, some of whom were passed out in the toilets, others under tables and elsewhere. Unfortunately, Onkel Franz stuttered badly when nervous, which made having to explain something to drunks in times of stress especially challenging. With great difficulty he managed eventually to round up his men. I was with a bunch of other townspeople who had gathered by the fire station to watch the brigade come and save the farm.

When they finally arrived, Onkel Franz stopped in front of the building, gathered the men up and said to them in as stern a tone as he could muster: 'A-a-all-all-all men step up. One, t-t-t-two, thr-thr-thr-three!'

All took a step forward and saluted, then about-faced and marched into the building to fetch the cistern truck. The equipment had first to be pulled to the river to fill the cistern under my uncle's orders. There was a total of six volunteers plus my uncle, and as all of them had been drinking heavily they didn't get very far. The combination of inebriation and stuttering commands slowed the operation down so much that the troops finally showed up when the buildings had already burned to the ground – exactly as intended.

Sadly, the next morning, the corpse of a Brenkener friend of the family was found floating 30 or 40 kilometres downstream in another town. He had fallen into the treacherous River Alme the previous night during the *Schützenfest*. The river contained underwater tunnels that connected it to a network of other rivers and created a powerful undertow that would suck people under. The firemen always worried about this when getting into the river to fill the cistern. Unfortunately, since everybody was so drunk, nobody had noticed the man had gone missing. I felt his death keenly. Like me, he had served in the war, and it was sadly ironic that he should have survived the war only to trip over his own feet at a party and drown. Life was random and cruel.

Sometime later, the family whose farmhouse burnt down were summoned by an investigative commission to appear in court in the neighbouring town of Paderborn. Just about everybody in town, including myself, went along to witness proceedings and gawp at the courthouse. The farmers were asked to describe and account for their belongings. They gave a statement listing everything they had, down to tableware and spoons.

At one point the judge asked the woman on the stand, 'Did you have any works of art in your possession?'

'Yes, your honour, we had a valuable oil painting.'

'Ah,' exclaimed the judge. 'What did it look like?'

'The oil painting was under a thick layer of glass, it was. My husband made it into a pretty table-top,' she said with conviction.

At that point the judge understood what was meant by an 'oil painting'. Clearly, it was some sort of cheap print under glass, but the farmers thought that maybe the judge would grant them more money if they induced him to believe it was valuable.

I watched the proceedings with interest. The end of my year of forced farm labour was approaching, after which I would finally be able go home. I would go back to school eventually, and I didn't know what was going to happen then. My mind was confused. I had been feeling as if I had gone underwater and couldn't get back to the surface. But something about the courtroom caught my attention. The interaction between the judge and the farmers fascinated me. The judge had the task of evaluating whether these people were telling the truth. He asked probing, purposeful questions. Ultimately, he got to make an important decision that had real-life consequences. A fleeting thought crossed my mind. *Could I maybe do something like this judge one day?*

In the end, the judge found the farmers not guilty of purposely setting fire to their farmhouse, which meant they would collect their insurance money. The farmers celebrated, and everybody congratulated them on their good fortune. The verdict, although flawed in my opinion, did not change my mind about how impressed I was with what I had seen. There was a sense of order and logic in that courtroom that I had not seen elsewhere, and it appealed to me.

One could easily be annoyed by the farmers' bravado and trickery. On the surface, aside from the presence of the occupying troops, it appeared that they had not been touched by the war; indeed, if anything, they seemed to have profited from it. The landscape was untouched, as rural areas like this village, unlike the cities, had largely been spared the bombing, and Russian troops had not reached this part of Germany. There was no lack of food since it was a farming community and, but for a few things the farmers could not make themselves, there were no shortages.

But the farmers had paid a price, and that price was blood; the blood of fathers, husbands and sons who went to war and never returned. Hardly a family had not felt the sorrow of a loved one lost. Everybody's house had a little shrine, on the mantelpiece or a special desk fitted out for the purpose, with pictures of the dead, often the obituary picture side by side with photos of happier days, and a crucifix and candle, always lit in remembrance. My Tante Gertrud and Onkel Franz Bach had lost two sons in Russia, and the third was a prisoner of war, working in the mines in France. Tante Thea had lost her husband, Onkel Joseph, and she was left with nobody, because they had no children. Onkel Konrad had lost his only son at the Russian front. The war had collected its dues even here.

Chapter 31

Return from the Farm

My mother called Onkel Franz at the farm – he had installed a telephone – and announced, 'Franz, school has started again, so Willi has to come back home to go back to school right away, and that's that.'

The communist official at the Witten town hall who had stamped my farm labour papers could have tried to postpone my release from duty until late summer to make me complete the full year I had been given, but he was no longer at his post. As a result, no successful argument could be brought by anybody in a position of authority to keep me there any longer, and Onkel Franz had no choice but to let me go. Therefore, in early June 1946, soon after the *Schützenfest*, I got on the train in Brenken with the same tattered little suitcase I had with me when I first arrived, and finally left the farm behind.

Before boarding the train, I stood on the platform for a moment and took it all in. The moment of deliverance I had anticipated for so long was here. It was an anticlimax, not the dramatic event I had pictured in my mind. Nobody offered to see me off at the station, no hugs or moist-eyed goodbyes were exchanged, and not even a thank-you was uttered for the work I had done. With just a quick hug from Tante Theresa and from Mia – 'All right then, Willi, take care of yourself, and say hello to your mother. Don't be a stranger and come and visit,' they said. 'Sure, Tante Theresa, I will do that,' was all I could come up with in response – and a sausage sandwich in my bag for the journey, I walked out of the farm and, as the door closed behind me, left behind a chapter of my life. It was unsettling to gain my freedom after a long period of captivity; nobody was there to give me orders any more. I almost felt the urge to return, like a bird which is let out of its cage and, overwhelmed by the big, intimidating world, then flies right back into it.

Don't panic, it's time to go. Arming myself with courage, I stepped on to the train.

During the long months I spent at the farm my mother managed to save enough money to get me some clothes, some of which she had sewn herself, and I actually had one full change of civilian clothing – a nice 'city' outfit consisting of a grey, long-sleeved shirt, a brown striped woollen sleeveless waistcoat, long grey trousers, one pair of new brown leather shoes, new socks and a new set of underwear. As I got on the train in my new clothes I couldn't help remembering the last time I had been on it, dressed in military fatigues, standing precariously on the narrow step outside the carriage and desperately hanging on to the handle with one hand. It felt as if a long time had passed, and yet, as I travelled the familiar route to Paderborn, then to Dortmund and then on in the little train to Witten past all the small rural towns, I realized nothing much had changed.

Although the towns of Brenken and Witten were relatively close, the trip still took a long time because they had not yet been able to repair the track destroyed by Allied bombing. As the train slowly ambled its way through the towns, the same devastated landscape I had left behind greeted me again. As I stared out of the window, mountains of rubble and bombed-out facades with black, gaping holes where windows should have been, gutted and empty, kept passing me by like scenes from a silent film. The world outside, as I had, had been stuck in a holding pattern.

It started raining, and I suddenly felt a chill.

We got to the station Witten-Annen, but I lived closer to the *Hauptbahnhof,* the main station, which was a good distance away. Nevertheless, I got off and started walking in the relentless drizzle. I needed time to think. I was walking back into my old life, except that my old life did not exist anymore; it had been annihilated before my very eyes. Yet what was expected of me was that I should erase what had happened from my mind. My elders had made that very clear; Germany was to never speak of 'it' ever again.

'Shut up and carry on,' they said to me in so many words when I tried to tell them what had happened to me, what I had seen and done, the wounds I had suffered, the pain I felt. First, Tante Mimi and Onkel Hermann were clearly uncomfortable listening to me and hurriedly changed the subject. Then my mother hushed me when I arrived from captivity. My father still didn't speak to me at all, and Onkel Franz, when I tried to tell him, sternly cut me off: 'We don't speak of those things, boy. Nobody wants to hear it, remember that. Just carry on.'

Carry on doing what? What the hell am I supposed to do now?

There were no instructions for 'moving on'. It was obvious from the untouched ruins around me that the world could not care less about us and certainly wasn't going to help. I could not see a path forward. All that surrounded me was the deafening silence of total defeat, the crushing weight of unspeakable shame, choking us into silence. Was all that we had learned to be unlearned? How did one do that?

I walked through largely deserted streets, getting my bearings from the layout and from memory. Nothing had changed much from the last time I had seen Witten in the late summer of 1945, when I was released from the military hospital and sent home to check in at City Hall. Time had stood still. I shivered, and a deep sadness came over me as I walked past the jagged ruins of building after destroyed building, stray dogs rooting among them. Here was the evidence you could not escape. The deep, gashing wounds of destruction were exposed around me, like the dead bodies that had lain bare and unburied on the battlefields I had left behind. I swallowed hard, struggling to suppress the emotions that were washing over me in waves, threatening to overwhelm me. It all came rushing back – the SS executing my classmate, the Russian boy's eyes before I shot him, the exposed entrails of the dead nuns, the lynch mob, the visceral hate in Frank's eyes. The scream got stuck in my throat. *Why? Why did any of this have to happen?*

These feelings could not be allowed to resurface. It was just a sign of weakness. *Stop feeling sorry for yourself and live with it.* I closed my eyes, took a deep breath to regain my composure as best I could and kept walking.

Since our house had been destroyed, my parents were assigned an apartment in the Hochstrasse, across from the Schlosspark, which was a very short distance from the firm Klatsch GmbH, where the parents of my friend Kalla had their electronics business. I had not seen Kalla since I was sent away with the KLV, the children's relocation programme. He did not go, and I didn't know why he hadn't or where he was now. I reached the store and peered through the window. The store was closed. There were no TVs then, but they had radios and a few other things, although there wasn't much on display in the dusty, shabby little window, and the stuff that was in it looked like it had been there for a long time. I knocked, hoping against hope that a friendly face would materialize, but nobody came to the door. I kept on walking in the intensifying rain, moisture-swollen clouds darkening the sky.

As I continued up the Hochstrasse, our apartment was on the left-hand side. It was a drab, grey, nondescript building with rows of small windows that looked like the multiple beady eyes of a giant insect. I entered the building and walked up the dark, dank-smelling staircase. The only daylight came from a couple of narrow, yellow-tinted windows close to the ceiling that gave everything a sickly hue. I paused for a moment on the second-floor landing to collect my thoughts. What was I supposed to do and how was I supposed to act? Was I just expected to greet my mother cheerfully and settle in, as if nothing was the matter? *What is she going to say?* I knew she was waiting for me. Papa would be at work until later. She had been able to visit me a few times while I was at the farm, since after all my uncle couldn't very well prevent his own sister from seeing her son, but the time she could spend with me was always granted reluctantly and cut short under some pretence. Uncle Franz always wanted to keep his free farmhand busy and minimize any distractions that might give me ideas of freedom. After all, I had been ordered there by the authorities and, in true German fashion, it was understood that the authorities could not be disobeyed.

Mama would probably be overjoyed and make a fuss over me.

Did she bake me a cake? Shit, whatever you do, don't cry…

I stood in front of the door. My left hand was gripping the handle of my little suitcase so tightly that its seams bit into my palm. I looked at my right hand, calloused and red from hard labour and shaking slightly. Instead of a weapon or a hoe, this hand now was going to be expected to handle a fountain pen again, as I sat obediently at a desk in a classroom, picking up where I had left off before I descended into the hell of war. I closed my hand into a fist and knocked. I heard quick footsteps, almost running, and the door opened wide.

'My Willi! You're finally home, finally, finally!' she shouted and pulled me into a tight embrace, as if she never wanted to let me go again.

I cried. And she had baked a cake.

'Oh my, you are soaking wet, you poor child. I'll get you a towel. Sit down at the table and eat. You must be starving,' she urged me as I got inside and put down my suitcase in the hallway.

Food was the gift of comfort. I knew they had saved ration stamps, stood in long queues and probably called in some favours with the relatives at the farms to get the ingredients for the meal of a fat pork roast with red beets and steamed potatoes swimming in butter that my mother had prepared to celebrate my arrival. The aroma of it permeated the whole apartment. Oh yes, and there was a delicious pound cake, made with real flour. Mama could be very tenacious. I could just imagine her talking to the baker: 'Well, Herr Bäcker

['Mr Baker'], this just won't do, and I am not leaving here until I get some flour. My son is coming back from captivity, and we have been loyal customers of yours through thick and thin, even when you had nothing but *Ersatzbrot* to sell.' The baker had probably cringed and dug into his private supply just to get rid of her.

Mama carried on an animated chatter about where everything was located in the apartment, how everybody was doing, and all the plans for my return to school. Any mention of the past was carefully avoided, as I expected.

The place was a tiny one-bedroom apartment, with a small kitchen containing a table and three chairs. Thank God, my parents had got three beds from somewhere. In the single bedroom there were two beds for them pushed together and placed sideways, while mine was facing the wall so I would not have to look at them. They had been able to buy me a small desk and a chair to do my schoolwork, for which there was space under the kitchen window. They had ordered it from a carpenter who had built it with a fold-down tray. When I worked at my desk, I had the tray pulled up, and when I wasn't using it, I could fold it down, so that there was space in the kitchen again to walk around. I was grateful for everything my parents had done to make me comfortable, knowing how hard it must have been to get anything done in this paralyzed town without supplies or money. At the same time, my heart fell at the thought of starting over again with real school where I had left off, that July day in 1943 when the train took us away from our families to the KLV camps. Bridging that gap seemed insurmountable.

There was no running water in the apartments. There were three tenants on our floor: us, then next door a working-class family whose son was in the navy, and across the hall a single man. At the end of the hall was the communal bathroom consisting of a single toilet where we all had to do our business. That was the only place in the building with plumbing. If you needed water, you would take a bucket and go fill it from a tap on the wall next to the toilet. Every day I would carry a bucket there, fill it with water and take it to the kitchen to my mum, who used it to wash the dishes.

When she was done she would call from the kitchen, 'Willi, get the bucket.'

I would then go back and dump the water in the toilet. It only happened once a day because we only had one meal apart from breakfast, so there wasn't a lot to wash.

Nothing else got washed much. To wash ourselves, we stood in a tin bath that was set on the kitchen floor once a week. Mama heated water in a pan on the stove, and we poured it over our heads with a small, dented, white-enamelled metal cup, using a rag and a little bar of glycerin soap to wash with. I did not like this routine and tried to get it over with quickly because it was always so cold on account of our having no heating fuel. Mama used the same tin bath and glycerin soap to wash clothes. Everything had multiple uses. Nothing could be wasted.

I soon understood this was how things were going to be for us from now on. There was no way back to the way things were, and no way forward that I could discern. The freedom, the normal life I had yearned for, was becoming a bleak reality of permanent poverty and hopelessness. There was no future, no hope. Despite my efforts to hold it at bay, the darkness increased its grip on my mind.

Chapter 32

Holding Pattern

The neighbour who lived across from us was a graphic artist. Later that year, he painted a portrait of me. It showed me as I was then, a young man of sixteen with bright red hair wearing a brown striped waistcoat, my one and only city outfit. Mama was impressed with the painting and proudly hung it on the wall in the hallway. It was our only picture. The other neighbours, the working-class family, were the Schmidts. They had a son two or three years older than me who was a humorous character, always making jokes that were actually funny and made me laugh. I liked that. He was a sailor in the merchant marine. Schmidt Junior always wore his sailor's trousers with wide bell bottoms, which I secretly admired. We would often go out into town together and walk around, looking for something to do. My parents had bought me a pair of nice shiny leather boots for my sixteenth birthday, and I proudly sported them all the time around Witten. I also owned one coat, which I wore almost every day because it rained pretty much all the time.

Schmidt Junior and I would stroll up the Hochstrasse to the market, he in his bell bottoms and I in my shiny leather boots, trying to act important and managing to get what we liked to think were a few envious looks from passers-by. We grew close for the short time my parents and I lived at the rented apartment. He and I discussed many things, but we almost never spoke about the war. We carefully avoided the subject, although we mentioned it once.

'Did you serve?' I asked.

'Yeah, *Kriegsmarine* [Navy], North Atlantic. You?'

'Yeah, *Heer* [Army], Anti-Tank, Eastern Front.'

We gave each other a silent look of acknowledgment, locking eyes for a few seconds, and nodded briefly. I knew then that he understood, because I had seen in his eyes that he had experienced the war. I wondered what his private pain might be, his personal nightmares, what things he had seen that could not be unseen. But that was a luxury we didn't have. Talking about it was taboo. Nevertheless, it felt good to have a comrade who knew, who had been there. I took what comfort I could from that, knowing that I was not alone.

My favourite thing to do when I was not hanging out with Schmidt Junior was to go past the market down to the Widerstrasse to see the Schüttes, who were from my mother's side of the family but lived in the city and ran a business. I liked to spend time with Tante Anne and Onkel Paul and their kids, three boys who were my first cousins. Although they were all younger than me, the eldest, Yüppi, six years my junior, in time became one of my best friends. We enjoyed playing football in the back yard, as we had before I was sent away. I had often thought about these games when I was in the war and wished I were back here. Now that I was back, it was one of the few activities that could take my mind off things.

The goalposts were a couple of empty metal cans, and the ball was so deflated it didn't roll much, but we didn't let that stop us.

After a match, Tante Anne would call in her big booming voice, '*Jungens*, come inside and get something warm in your stomachs.'

She always had hot chicory ersatz coffee waiting for us, accompanied by a small piece of day-old brown bread we could dip in the fake coffee to make it soft and soggy.

Sometimes I would go further up the Hochstrasse through the underpass to the Herbergestrasse, where my Tante Mimi and Onkel Hermann, the butcher, lived, and I would visit my Oma. She was a very devout Catholic, and every time I visited her she would ask me,

'Willi, did you go to church today?' and I would answer, 'Yes, that is where I am coming from. I was at the meditation this afternoon.'

She was quite satisfied with that answer.

'That's a good boy, Willi' she would nod approvingly, patting my hand.

There wasn't much to be happy about in those days, and this was a little thing I could do for her. Tante Mimi and Onkel Herman were in on it and winked and nodded at me, and I chuckled and winked back. It made me feel better, too, for a little while.

School at the *Oberschule für Jungen*, the boys' secondary school, had finally resumed in January 1946. I had missed the first months of teaching because of my conscription at the farm. My mother had managed to extract me in June to prevent my missing too much school, and as instruction was so spotty, I hadn't missed much at all. We shared the school with the girls, whose building was partly destroyed, partly occupied by Allied administrators. We alternated the lesson time, no more than thirteen hours a week in total, between mornings and afternoons, as there was a severe shortage of teachers. Those like me, whose school career had been damaged academically by Hitler's dogmatic and deficient teaching directives during the war years and who were ultimately pulled into the war, had to be reincorporated into mainstream instruction and brought up to speed with remedial courses, which presented special challenges.

Most of the school itself had not been bombed, although the gym and indoor pool had been destroyed, as had the *Aula*, the performance hall. As there was no paper available, we had to write our lessons on the margins of scraps of newspaper we collected in the neighbourhood. All the windows in the classrooms were broken, with no hope of being replaced, and heating fuel was unavailable. The old school archives and many excellent books fell victim to the furnace during the winter of 1946 to provide what little heat they could produce to keep us from freezing. When it was cold we had to wear our coats, scarves, caps and gloves in class. Lessons were cut to about twenty minutes in winter because it was so cold that our fingers would no longer work properly. When I got home I could often not make out what I had written.

Hunger was still our constant companion. My mother kept the food ration stamps organized in a large wallet. They came in cards with multiple stamps printed on them. Each type of card had its own colour: red for butter and fat, yellow for milk, and so on. It made it easier for housewives to pull the right card out when they went to the market. Most foods could only be purchased with ration stamps. Only a few seasonal vegetables, like onions or beets, could be bought without them. At the beginning of every month my mother had to go with her identification card and money to get new ration stamps. If she ran out of stamps during the month she had to wait until the next month to be issued with more, so she had to be creative to produce meals with the limited amount and variety of food available.

Having a ration card did not guarantee the availability of the item. Often she would come back from the market empty-handed after having waited in a long queue for hours, only to find out that they had run out of the stuff before she had her turn. That is where the family at the farm came in, providing some much-needed extras, because people could barely live on the rations alone. I realized then that this helped explain the limited resistance my parents had posed to the treatment I had received at the hands of Onkel Franz. They had been, and still were, dependent on handouts from the farm to survive, particularly in winter. It all made sense now.

'Mama, is that why you didn't really argue with Onkel Franz when he treated me so badly?' I asked.

She hung her head. 'Yes, son, I am sorry. We depend on them for food.'

Sitting at the kitchen table, in a rare moment of vulnerability she started confiding in me how hard it had been: the war, the air raids, the hunger, the constant worry of not knowing whether I was alive or dead. She told me about how our friends had all fared. That is when I asked her something that had been weighing on me for a long time.

'Mama, what happened to the Rosenbaums? I remember I couldn't go see Fritz anymore, but nobody ever told me why. Was it because his dad is a Jew? Where are they now?'

She paused, collecting herself.

'Yes, son, it was because Herr Rosenbaum was a Jew. We were forbidden to fraternize. Especially with your father being a government employee, he would have lost his job, and much worse …'

She stopped for a moment, looking at her hands.

'Frau Rosenbaum was told to divorce her husband, but she refused to leave him. Eventually, in 1943, Herr Rosenbaum was sent to a concentration camp, Theresienstadt. Frau Rosenbaum was left behind with Fritz, ineligible for food stamps, reduced to accepting charity, which nobody could actually give her since it was forbidden to help Jews and their families.'

I sat glued to my chair, absorbing with mounting dread the words that were coming out of my mother's mouth. So it was true, at least some of it. We really had done some of the horrible things the American soldiers at the internment camp said we did. I had refused to believe the fantastic tales of the acts of cruelty and barbarism the Allied soldiers accused us of committing, and had rejected the awful pictures they had shown us, dismissing them as lies. It just couldn't be. A knot formed in my stomach as I listened, bringing on a cold wave of nausea.

'At first, I slipped her some food stamps. I would leave a newspaper on the porch with the stamps inside, and she would scoop up the paper when she passed in front of the house. Then, when it got really bad, I hid her and little Fritz in our coal cellar.'

'And Herr Rosenbaum?' I managed to ask, afraid of the answer.

'Luckily, Herr Rosenbaum survived, and he has returned to Witten, thank the Lord. Can you believe it? He wants to reopen the shoe store.'

'Oh, Mama, that's great.'

I was so excited my eyes were watering; finally, some good news had penetrated through the fog of depressing events. I felt a small glimmer of optimism. Maybe things could turn around after all. If Rosenbaum could think of rebuilding his life after all that had happened to him, then perhaps so could I. But as soon as I formulated the thought, the shadow of my mother's revelations extinguished it. We were the bad guys. There was no redemption for us, and I was guilty by association. What had we done? How could anybody forgive us? The darkness in my mind spread its tendrils farther into my consciousness.

* * *

I mostly felt as if I was a burden to my parents. But I was able to make one small contribution to improving their lives. The food situation at home changed slightly for the better because I had my Rucksack with the cartons of cigarettes I got when my unit raided the German military depot on our way to the front. Cigarettes were currency you could use in the black market to get things you needed. One cigarette alone could buy you one egg or 50gm of meat. I had to ration the cigarettes carefully, since nobody knew how long this deprivation was going to last, but they did provide some relief when it was most urgent.

My father and I had not really spoken since the day I encountered him on the street when I returned from the war. Since I returned home we had settled into an uncomfortable routine of mostly avoiding each other, but that was difficult in the small apartment. My father could not help but notice that sometimes, after having been out during the day, I was bringing home food items and other necessities I knew we badly needed

'What do you have there?' he asked as I walked in one evening with my Rucksack looking bulky.

'I got some milk and butter, and some eggs,' I replied, my back stiffening.

He raised his eyebrows. 'Let me see.'

I set my pack down on the kitchen table and opened it to take out the food. As I did so, he saw the cartons of cigarettes and his eyes widened.

'Where did you get that?'

'Doesn't matter. I brought it home because it can help us.'

'Hmm, I see. Well … that's good, I … suppose … your mother will be happy. Go on and tell her.'

He walked away abruptly and headed out of the door.

After that, he started taking a more active interest when I brought something home, and we would briefly talk about what I had and what was needed in the house.

'Do you think you can find shoe polish?' he asked quietly one evening, looking at the ground.

I followed his gaze and looked at the one pair of formal shoes he wore to work every day. I saw how scuffed and worn they were, the brown leather faded to yellow in some places, the sides looking frayed, the toes almost completely rubbed off. He cut out newspaper pages and used them as liners to insulate his feet from the holes in the soles.

'I'll see what I can find.' I looked away, trying to sound casual.

I found some brown polish in the black market a couple of days later.

'I got the polish,' I told him as I walked into the kitchen.

His face lit up when I took it out of the Rucksack. He walked silently to a cabinet, took out two rags and spread one out on the kitchen table. Then he sat down, took off his shoes and placed them on one of the rags. He unscrewed the top of the polish jar, dipped the other rag in it and started applying the polish to his shoes with the utmost care and concentration.

Slowly, like the shoes, our relationship began to mend.

* * *

One day, they opened a cinema in Witten in the area where Tante Mimi lived, close to the wall where I saw my father the day I returned from the war. They were showing a British film in English with German subtitles. It was in colour and had to do with witches. The title was 'Ghost', or something like that. My friends from school had managed to get tickets and we could hardly contain our excitement. We stood in a long queue, happily suffering the bone-chilling drizzle, coat collars turned up, giddy that we had a chance to see this amazing new show.

'This is going to be soo good,' one of my friends said.

'Yes, but don't drool all over yourself now,' somebody retorted, trying to act all calm and collected, but the truth was we were all jumping out of our skins in anticipation.

We entered the darkened cinema and quietly took our seats. The moment the screen came down we were glued to it, our eyes grew ever wider. We had never seen a film in colour, and it took our breath away. The plot didn't matter, it was the vividness of the images on the screen that held us in a trance. I was used to the British English accent so it was no problem for me to understand the dialogue, and this meant I didn't need to read the subtitles or take my eyes off the colour images.

That was the first time since the war that we had had a real distraction, when we could, for a brief moment, forget our situation. Forget for just an instant the devastation outside. Forget the apocalyptic time that was our reality.

Chapter 33

The Path Forward

I was two grades behind where I should have been because of the war. There were thirteen grades altogether in German schools, after which we took the *Abitur* exam to gain a high school diploma and entrance to university. I would be twenty-one years old by the time I graduated. A group of us, the 'damaged' ones, were taking the remedial classes which were threatening to put us even further behind our original classmates. I didn't know where I was headed, or if I was going anywhere at all. Everything around me was at a standstill, and no help was forthcoming. I could not concentrate, nor was I interested in the school subjects, or anything else. My marks were terrible, and my parents were becoming concerned, not knowing how to help me.

As I came to learn later, I had missed the *Entnazifizierung*, the denazification campaign held at school while I was at the farm. Consequently, I lacked some context others had acquired in the meantime, which made things more difficult for me to understand. I knew we had lost the war and were being punished, but I struggled to grasp why the punishment was so severe as to withhold food from the population and actively prevent reconstruction, or why so many seemed to hate us so much. The reports about the appalling treatment of the Jews had sounded incredible to me, and I had resisted believing them, but the story Mama told me about the Rosenbaums was inescapably real. I knew then, despite my reluctance, that I had to accept the haunting truth. That meant that I also had to accept that my reality, my entire life, had been an illusion, under which lurked a dark and disturbing underbelly of evil. What, then, could I believe in anymore? I had become unmoored.

Nobody talked about the war, and the silence weighed me down to a point where I could feel it like a physical weight on my chest. Everything we had been taught in kindergarten and primary school, that the Führer was our saviour and we owed him everything, that we Germans were better than anybody else and others were out to cheat us and take what was rightfully ours, turned out to be a web of lies. Healthy, traditional values had been twisted into sick propaganda and fed to us. I was complicit by association in crimes I couldn't even comprehend.

As I listened to the teachers and the news over the course of the year, I slowly pieced things together and reached the conclusion that I had only survived by accident. I had not been expected to live. My comrades and I were knowingly and purposely sent by our leaders to our deaths to prolong the existence of the Reich by a few more months. We had been used. We had been robbed of our innocence and our childhoods. Many more had been robbed of their very existence. Now, in school, we were told to unlearn everything, by some of the very same teachers who had previously extolled the virtues of the Führer to us. We were supposed to become obedient world citizens who would embrace democracy and put the past behind us. That sounded great, but when were our teachers lying to us, then or now? Did they lie to us about the virtues of the Führer then because they had to, or did they believe in him? Were they lying now about how they felt about democracy? How could I trust any of them? My blood boiled when I thought of the role I had been duped into playing in this corrupt play of power, and I couldn't shake off the feeling.

It was in this frame of mind that I found myself one chilly morning in late September 1947 standing with my mates in the schoolyard at break. We were huddled together in a tight circle, shivering and blowing on our hands while smoking cigarettes, trying in vain to extract some warmth from the glowing sticks. Minors were technically not allowed to smoke on school premises, but the rule was never enforced. We were also holding little containers of chocolate milk, served daily at school as a dietary supplement which the Allied Forces had started providing. Suddenly, out of the corner of my eye, I spied the principal, Herr Noelle, rapidly approaching us. He seemed agitated.

He planted himself in a wide stance behind me and barked, 'Langbein! Drop the cigarette!'

Slightly bewildered, I started turning toward him as I took a drag. Then, without warning, his hand came flying across my face, knocking the cigarette clean out of my mouth. A split second later, my fist landed squarely on his nose, the little milk carton I had been holding flying into the air and spraying everybody nearby with a brown sticky mist. He tumbled backwards, stunned, holding his bloody nose.

I got right up to him, looked him in the eye and spat, 'Oh, so I am not old enough to smoke a cigarette, but I was old enough to put my life on the line for the likes of you? Kiss my arse!'

Then I stormed out of the school. Enough was enough. I was ready to burst. I couldn't take it anymore.

In the end, the official punishment I received was a formal letter of reprimand for wasting government-issued milk, admonishing me that it was a serious infraction to squander valuable resources meant for the students' proper nutrition and well-being, an infraction which, if repeated, could lead to suspension or expulsion from school. My father had to acknowledge receipt of the letter. I really didn't care, but he never commented on it.

I stopped going to school regularly. Nightmares woke me up every night. I stayed in bed most of the day, unable to function. I was angry at the world; angry that I had been deceived and used; angry that they put us in harm's way and destroyed our world and our futures; angry that so many people had died and my name was forever associated with unthinkable atrocities; angry at God for allowing this to happen. I punched the walls of my room like a madman, terrifying my parents. Waves of anguish washed over me and paralyzed me. What was the point of carrying on? I slipped into the dark place that I had held at bay for so long.

For weeks I drifted in and out of despair.

Somewhere in the back of my mind I knew I couldn't go on hiding indefinitely. I couldn't be a burden to my parents. I owed it to them to pull myself together because I was all they had. They were going to need me to take care of them when they got old. It was my duty as a son not to give up and fail them, and that obligation was as true now as it had been before the war. I had found my anchor. But how to carry on was something I couldn't yet answer.

Friends from school had told me about sports associations. I decided to try one out to shake off the gloom and I joined a sports group called VFB Witten. It felt like a way to pass the time and distract from the dreariness of my life. It turned out to be therapeutic for me, as it temporarily cleared my mind of the constant misery of my thoughts. I played handball for a while as a goalkeeper, until at some point I grew tired of it and became interested in joining the football team. I started playing as a goalie, thinking it would be similar to handball, but having only ever played football with my cousins in the back yard, I didn't know much about the rules of the game. I found out rather quickly that it was very different from handball and that being a football goalkeeper was not at all the same thing. In the beginning the opposing forwards put shots past me as if I wasn't even there. This was embarrassing; I had thought myself a decent handball goalie, but now I was getting walloped. My competitiveness soon kicked in, however, and I endeavoured to master this new skill. It gave me something to concentrate on, to let off steam.

After the war, the British troops had a non-fraternization rule. There was to be no personal contact between the occupying forces and the civilian population. This prohibition was soon relaxed, and completely lifted at some point in 1946, and relationships started developing between the British occupying troops and German civilians. Soon after the ban was lifted, the German-English youth club association was founded, of which I became the deputy chairman, helped in no small part by my good command of the English language. A British sergeant major named Charles was the chair of the organization. He was young, in his early twenties. Charles took an interest in me, and we started having long conversations that I found engaging in a way that nothing else had been for a long time.

'Your English is very good, Willi. You could use this talent to your advantage. As Germany is rebuilt, Germans with good English skills will be needed.'

'Why do you think that? What could I do?' I asked, interested.

'Well, the whole country and its new democratic system of government is being developed. You could be part of that development; there will be a lot of job opportunities in government. You're a bright fellow, you could represent your country.'

Nobody had ever really talked like that to me, with ideas for the future. I became fascinated with the notions Charles was planting in my head, about rebuilding Germany and the thought that I could somehow play a part in it.

We soon started playing football at the association, the Germans against the Tommies. I thought I had learned enough about the game at the sports club, but when I went in goal during the first match, the Tommies promptly put ten goals past me, and Charles had a good laugh at my expense.

Charles went horse-riding, which I thought was grand. One day, he rode over to pay my family a visit at the Ruhrstrasse 51, our new apartment with its own toilet situated above the Klatsch family's electronics store, a big improvement after the dingy old place with the communal bathroom and no running water. It was in an old nineteenth century building, which still had hooks outside the door to which you could tie your horse. Charles promptly secured his mount and came up the stairs. He brought gifts for my mother, English chocolate and Nescafé, luxuries we had never experienced before. He showed us how Nescafé was prepared in England, not with water but with milk.

'Could you ask your mother if she could heat up some milk?' he asked me, as his German was insufficient.

I explained to Mama what needed to be done. While the milk was on the stove, she pulled out three nice china cups she still had and carefully placed them on saucers. We waited expectantly for the next step.

'Now pour the milk into the cups.'

My mother obliged. Then he unscrewed the top of the clear glass Nescafe container, took out a spoonful of the coffee granules and dropped them into one of the cups, stirring them into the milk, which released a heavenly aroma that flooded our deprived senses. Charles offered the steaming cup to my mother.

Ach, Herr Offizier, sehr galant,' she crowed, cheeks flushed in excitement.

'*Gern geschehen, meine Dame,*' he replied in his heavily accented German, which she found even more charming.

She glowed, and it made me feel warm inside to see her smile with such genuine happiness. It got me thinking that perhaps, despite everything, we could all still learn to look forward to better things to come.

His visit made a lasting impression on Mama.

'Willi, you must invite your nice British friend to the house again,' she demanded.

Papa was less enthusiastic. He still had a difficult time seeing the former enemy as a 'liberator', but he was also clear-headed about Germany's situation and understood how cultivating a friendship with a British soldier might be beneficial to his son's chances. He also knew that Germany only had a future as an integral part of Europe, forming strong alliances with its neighbours, and on this point he agreed with Charles. He knew only too well, having lived through two world wars, that there was no other option. My father would remain scarred by the catastrophic failures of the German state that had defined his entire life, but he held out hope that his son's future could be brighter.

Charles and I developed a bond. I taught him German, and he taught me English. He did visit my parent's house again on several occasions and had discussions with my father about Germany's incipient reconstruction, sanctioned by President Truman under his new order, JCS 1779, issued in July 1947, officially authorizing the economic recovery of Germany.

At seventeen years old I was ready for these serious talks. We talked at length about world events, mostly Charles talking and me trying to absorb the information I found so fascinating. Perhaps he thought of me like a younger brother in need of guidance. The conversations I had with him sparked something inside of me. Through his eyes I saw a much bigger picture of a world I had not really known existed.

'Wouldn't it be grand to see a union of countries, where resources could be shared and every country could achieve a good standard of living?' I asked, inspired by our talks.

Charles smiled and nodded. 'Yes, that would be grand indeed. And wouldn't it be great if we had a hand in it?'

Gradually, hope made its way back into my heart and mind, lifting the veil of darkness ever so slightly. I started to glimpse a way forward for myself and for my country, both fates solidly intertwined in my mind. And I decided it was up to me to work out how to get there.

Spurred on by this Anglo-German friendship, the idea of participating in the creation of a better Germany took hold of me. At school I had just learned the concept that the whole is greater than the sum of its parts, and it made sense to me when I applied it to the idea of a coalition of countries. My father was urging me to go to university and work for the German government – *Vater Staat*, Father State, as he called it. 'Willi, the State will always take care of you,' he liked to say – and Charles was saying that maybe I could get a job in government to be part of this big change.

My head started filling up with possibilities, fuzzy as they were, still lacking true direction or definition; but something in me had shifted. I had found inspiration. Soon I became fuelled by a desire to pursue this dream. I decided I would study law and become like that judge in Brenken who had so impressed me. I thought that perhaps I could help to make good laws for my country.

As I sat at home in late 1947, doing homework at the school desk my father had so thoughtfully commissioned for me the year before, I could finally see a future beyond the ruins. I knew then already without a doubt that I would do this thing. I didn't know how just yet, but I was determined to play my part in making my country better, and to ensure that the evil I had witnessed was never repeated.

* * *

What I didn't know then was that the vision of a unified Europe would come true with the creation of NATO in 1949, and later with the founding of the European Union, which Germany joined. I didn't know that I would work in the dangerous furnaces of the Ruhr Valley steel foundries every summer to pay my way through college to become a lawyer, or that I would get married to a lovely Spanish woman and have two beautiful daughters who brightened my life.

I didn't know then that I would join the German Department of Defence and take an assignment in Paris with ESRO, the European Space Research Organization, where I would work to promote collaborative relationships between the partner states. Or, that on 28 February 1979 in Paris, I would receive the bronze medal of European Merit, for my contribution to furthering the goal of building a democratic and unified Europe, from a representative of the European Union, the lawyer François Visine, founder and president of the Order of European Merit. He was Foreign Affairs Minister of Luxembourg and later became the vice-president of his country. I didn't know then that I would spend the last years of my career as the head of Germany's NATO legal contracts division NEFMA, or that I would draw up the contract for the NATO forces fighter jet, the Tornado, which is still in operation today.

I could not know any of this then, but as I sat daydreaming at my desk I remembered the words my Opa Johannes spoke to me one summer afternoon long ago when I was a little boy and we were standing together in the wheat fields. When I asked him, filled with hope and apprehension, if I could ever become a dowser like him, he squeezed my hand, looked down at me with a big smile and said, '*Ja*, little Willi, it's easy. You can do anything. You just have to believe you can.'

Epilogue

The bronze medal of European Merit for my father's contributions to furthering the goal of building a democratic and unified Europe hangs on the living room wall at my parents' home in Spain. On it, the goddess Europa is seen riding a bull. My father used to complain that he only got the bronze medal and not the silver or gold because he refused to travel more, wishing understandably to spend time with his family, and he was very disappointed not to have received the higher award. Next to the medal hangs the portrait of my father at sixteen painted in 1946 by the artist who lived across the hallway from his parent's apartment.

My father spent his entire professional life on foreign assignments for the German Department of Defence, moving his family from country to country in the process. This afforded my mother, my sister and me a broad world view, the gift of many languages and an understanding of different peoples and cultures, all of which I am immensely grateful for to this day. My father also taught me to live by high ethical standards. Leading by example, he never compromised his integrity, even though it often meant taking the more difficult road.

He passed away on 3 January 2018. Until the end of his life he believed in the strength of a unified Europe, but he became increasingly concerned about the geopolitical events unfolding during the last years of his life. Since his death, I have felt a growing sense of urgency to share his story with others.

We are seeing a resurgence of nationalism, populism, neo-fascism and neo-nazism in multiple countries around the world, including the United States. My father's tale is a stark reminder of the consequences extremist political movements can have. If he were alive today, he would warn that the rhetoric of intolerance and hatred these factions spread is destructive of democracy. Countries that harbour this cancer see their moral values misused and eventually disintegrating. Nazi Germany not only wrought destruction on multiple countries and ethnic groups in its delusional imperialistic quest for racial hegemony – most notably and tragically on Jews, but also on the Romani and the Sinti people, the disabled, gays, trade unionists, political dissenters, members of the clergy, and many more – it almost destroyed itself and its own people in so doing. My father, taken from his family as a child to be sent into battle to die in a war that was already lost, is an example of this wanton self-destruction, and of the devastating consequences suffered when authoritarianism gains the upper hand and eliminates the freedoms we take for granted today.

Perhaps my father's account can remind us not to succumb to the temptation to believe aspiring tyrants when they play on our frustrations and our fears and present themselves as the sole source of truth and key to the ultimate solution.

Bibliography

Sources available online

Ash, Lucy. 'The Rape of Berlin' BBC News, Berlin, 1 May 2015. https://www.bbc.com/news/magazine-32529679

Chen, C. Peter. 'Battle of Vienna, 2 April 1945 – 13 April 1945.' *World War II Database*. (2012): n. pag. https://ww2db.com/battle_spec.php?battle_id=285

Delvaux de Fenffe, Gregor. 'Deutsche Geschichte, Flucht und Vertreibung'. Planet Wissen. (2020) n. pag. https://www.planet-wissen.de/geschichte/deutsche_geschichte/flucht_und_vertreibung/index.html

'Deutsches Jungvolk.' Wikipedia (2021) https://de.wikipedia.org/wiki/Deutsches_Jungvolk

'Engines of the Red Army in WWII'. https://www.o5m6.de/redarmy_old/BattleOfVienna.html

'Forced Labour of Germans after WWII.' *Wikipedia*. https://en.wikipedia.org/wiki/Forced_labor_of_Germans_after_World_War_II

Lukasch, Peter. 'Der muss haben ein Gewehr: Krieg, Militarismus und patriotische Erziehung in Kindermedien.' Kinder und Jugendliteratur von 1900 bis 1960. (2021) http://www.zeitlupe.co.at/werbung/propaganda2.html

Maier-Bode, Sine. *Kindheit im ZweitenWeltkrieg. Kinderlandverschickung.* Planet Wissen. (2004). https://www.planet-wissen.de/geschichte/nationalsozialismus/kindheit_im_zweiten_weltkrieg/pwiekinderlandverschickung100.html

Pezzei, Kristina. 'Viele kamen nicht zurück', *Stern*, 14 March 2005. https://www.stern.de/politik/geschichte/kriegsgefangene-viele-kamen-nicht-zurueck-3548272.html

Reynolds, Major General Michael. 'A Soviet Red Army Victory at Vienna.' Warfare History Network. (2009) n. pag. Available: https://warfarehistorynetwork.com/daily/wwii/a-soviet-red-army-victory-at-vienna/

Roth, Thomas. *1933–1945: Nazionalsozialismus und Zweiter Weltkrieg.* Portal Rheinischer Geschichte. http://www.rheinische-geschichte.lvr.de/Epochen-und-Themen/Epochen/1933-bis-1945---nationalsozialismus-und-zweiter-weltkrieg-/DE-2086/lido/57ab25d840b824.40615976

Struck, Bernhard. 'Die Hitlerjugend (HJ).' © Deutsches Historisches Museum, Berlin, 13 Mai 2015. Lebendiges Museum Online. https://www.dhm.de/lemo/kapitel/ns-regime/ns-organisationen/jugend/

Books

Balabkins, Nicholas. *Germany under Direct Controls: Economic Aspects of Industrial Disaramament 1945–1948.* New Brunswick, N.J.: Rutgers University Press, 1964

Beschloss, Michael. *The Conquerors: Roosevelt, Truman and the Destruction of Hitler's Germany, 1941–1945.* New York: Simon & Schuster, 2002

Eckhertz, Holger. *D-Day through German Eyes.* DTZ History Publications, 2015, 2016

Hoehne, Heinz. *The Order of the Death's Head: The Story of Hitler's SS.* London: Penguin Books, 2000

Lukasch, Peter. *Der muss haben ein Gewehr: Krieg, Militarismus und patriotische Erziehung in Kindermedien.* Norderstedt: BoD – Books on Demand, 2012

MacDonogh, Giles. *After the Reich: The Brutal History of the Allied Occupation.* New York: Basic Books, 2007

Schlessier, Karl Heinz. *Flakhelfer to Grenadier: Memoir of a Boy Soldier, 1943–1945.* West Midlands: Helion & Company Limited, 2014

Schoppmeyer, Heinrich. *Witten, Geschichte von Dorf, Stadt und Vororten.* Dortmund: Scholz-Druck und Medien service, 2012

Vuillard, Eric. *El Orden del Dia.* Barcelona: Tusquets Editores, 2018

Wiehe, Gerhard. *Die Penne 41–51: Oberschule für Jungen Witten 1941–1951.* Witten. Bommerbank Verlag, 1985